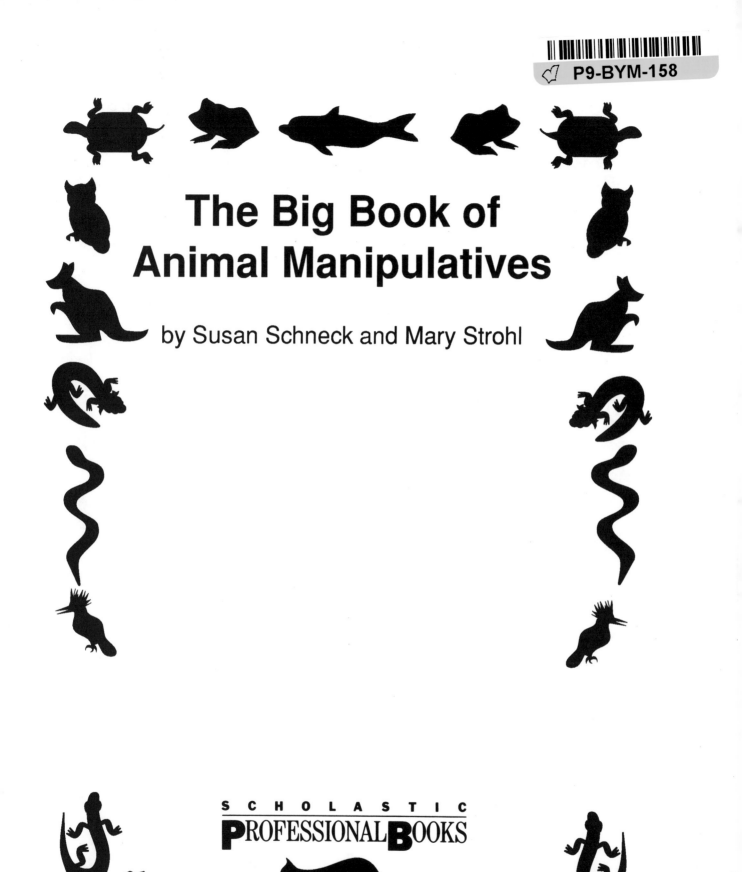

The Big Book of
Animal Manipulatives

by Susan Schneck and Mary Strohl

SCHOLASTIC
PROFESSIONAL BOOKS

New York • Toronto • London • Auckland • Sydney

About the Authors

Susan Schneck and Mary Strohl have many years combined experience in education and publishing. In 1986 they formed their own studio, Flights of Fancy, specializing in children's activity products and elementary teaching materials. In 1991 Mary moved to Durham, North Carolina with her husband, Harlan. Sue remains in Racine, Wisconsin with her husband, Bob, and their two daughters, Kate and Jenny. Mary and Sue continue their creative alliance via phone, FAX, and "working vacations." This is their fifth title for Scholastic Professional Books.

Many hours have been spent researching animals and working out worthwhile animal activities that are easy for teachers to reproduce and for children to construct. We hope these animal manipulatives will help young learners become more aware of many animals and stimulate them to find out more in the myriad of books and videos available.

Special Thanks to

Katherine Carson for her help in researching literature and other classroom resources.

George Gabriel for helping to illustrate the animals realistically and beautifully.

Harlan Strohl for experimenting in his garden with bird-feeder crafts.

Book design by Mary Strohl and Susan Schneck (Flights of Fancy)
Book illustrations by George Gabriel and Susan Schneck
Cover design by Vincent Ceci
Cover illustrations by Susan Schneck

ISBN 0-590-49245-4

Printed in the U.S.A.

Table of Contents

About This Book

The Big Book of Animal Manipulatives has easy-to-create animal activities, projects, and games adaptable for grades K-3. Children will put together and use activities that will encourage them to learn about animals: how they grow, and how they live in their habitats. Animal facts, teacher information, and instructions for using activities begin each chapter to help you create an atmosphere for learning about animals. Children will have fact wheels to turn, windows to peek under, cards and cubes to sort and match, finger puppets and scenes to create, and much more. The **Directory of Animal Manipulatives** in the back of the book is an easy reference for assembly of all the projects. The bibliography starting on page 142 will help you gather library books and other materials for use in your classroom studies.

All the activities are reproducible for individual, group, or classroom use. Chapters 1 through 4 have information and activities about **mammals, amphibians, reptiles, and birds**. Each chapter describes:

• what makes a group of animals special or different from other animals;
• animals in the wild;
• eating habits;
• and family life.

Chapter 5, **Animals and Their Habitats**, shows all the groups of animals in various habitats such as woodlands, rain forests, deserts, and more. Backgrounds and stand-up animal puppets help children to set the stage for learning about animal adaptation to climate and the food chain. This chapter also has ecology projects that will enable children to preserve natural habitats for animals and to help animals survive in our environments.

Setting the Stage for Learning

Each chapter begins with animal facts and teacher background for helping children learn about the different animal groups. Use the facts to stimulate discussion and to create big books, mini-books, posters, and bulletin boards. *The Big Book of Animal Manipulatives* is a supplement to other animal texts and books. Use the projects provided to enhance your own curriculum. The bibliography at the back of the book will help you gather materials about animal groups that are appropriate for use in your classroom. Your school or public librarian should be able to help you gather other materials.

When you have gathered various materials, whet the imaginations of your children by asking them to bring pictures of their own pets, animal books, and animal toys to school. Separate the pictures, books, or toys into the groups of animals you will be studying.

Using This Book

There are many cut, paste, and assemble activities in *The Big Book of Animal Manipulatives.* They are easy for you to reproduce for your class and some activities are repeated in different chapters. Once you have helped a child with a project in one chapter, he or she will be able to assemble a similar project in another. The amount of help needed will depend on your age group. You may want to assemble some of the projects yourself for younger children to manipulate. Refer to the **Directory of Animal Manipulatives** in the back of the book for directions for assembling all the activities. Instructions for specific use of each activity appears on the **Teacher Pages** at the beginning of each chapter. Note**:** For Fact Wheels, Picture Cubes and Match and Sort Cards, you may want to reproduce these similar projects in different pastel colors for each chapter. (For example: mammal projects on blue paper, reptiles on yellow, amphibians on green, birds on pink.) This will help to separate similar activities for different groups of animals. Identifying labels at the bottom of each page will be helpful in planning your course of study.

Starting with mammals in chapter one, reproduce, cut out, and color the large mammal examples on pages 8–10. Put them on a bulletin board or at the top of a big book page. Ask children to discuss the characteristics of mammals. Most children will be somewhat familiar with them. Building on prior knowledge helps children to gain confidence and eagerness for study. Peruse the **Mammal Facts** on page 5 to help you guide the children to look for certain traits of the mammals pictured. Let the children dictate facts as you write them down. When you feel they have enough information to proceed, start working on the activities. Your class does not have to work on every project to learn about animals. Choose the ones that are most appropriate to your class's abilities and needs. Learn as much as possible about mammals before moving on to amphibians.

Work on the amphibian projects in the same manner as with mammals before moving on to other chapters. This will help children learn about each group of animals in a logical manner. As they build their knowledge in each chapter, the class will begin to see how animal groups are similar or different. Add what you learn to your big books and bulletin boards. In Chapter 5, Animals and Their Habitats, the different animal groups will come together in varied environments and your class will see how the various animal groups interact.

Chapter 1: MAMMALS

Teacher: Use these facts with your class to stimulate discussion and to create big books, fact wheels, posters, and bulletin boards. Reproduce the facts chart below for children to use for reference.

What You Should Know About Mammals
- Mammals are the only animals with hair or fur.
- Mammals breathe with lungs.
- Mammals are warm blooded. Their temperature stays the same.
- Mammals have teeth. The shape of their teeth depends on the foods they eat.
- Mammals have large brains.
- Examples: person, lion, moose, whale

Mammals in the Wild
- Mammal hair can be in the form of hair or fur.
- Some mammals have hooves instead of toes (cow, horse, rhinoceros).
- Some mammals have antlers that they shed each year (deer, moose).
- Other mammals have horns that are never shed (bison, musk ox, eland).
- Mammals live in all sorts of environments (wetlands, deserts, oceans).
- Some mammals live on land (people, cats, deer, buffalo).
- Others mammals live in water (whale, porpoise, seal).
- Most mammals hunt for food in the daytime (elk, cow, kangaroo, goat).
- Some mammals come out of their homes only at night (opossum, armadillo).

Mammal Eating Habits
- Mammals use their teeth to grind or tear food.
- Some mammals eat only plants (*Herbivores*: giraffe, koala, llama, porcupine).
- Others eat only meat (*Carnivores*: hyena, lion, fox, dog).
- Some mammals eat both plants and meat (person, bear, coyote, gorilla).

Mammal Families
- Baby mammals look like miniature adults when they are born.
- Baby mammals are protected by their parents.
- Female mammals nurse their young with milk from their bodies.
- Parents teach babies how to hunt for food.
- Some mammals live alone after they are grown, and come together only to mate (bat, opossum, cuscus, squirrel).
- Other mammals live in family groups (raccoon, person, fox, seal, lion).

Teacher Page

The numbers shown after the titles indicate pages where patterns and assembly directions (**bold**) are found.

What You Should Know About Mammals

Big Book and Bulletin Board Mammals (pp. 8–10, **134**): Use the patterns on these pages to start your study of mammals. You may want to reduce or enlarge them to be more in proportion. The facts on the preceding page will help you guide classroom discussions.

Mammals in the Wild

Water Mammals Picture Cubes (pp. 11–12, **140**): Mammals that live in water are powerful swimmers with streamlined bodies and strong flippers. Their flippers are their legs. Water mammals feed on fish and other sea life. Some of these animals can hold their breath for long periods (e.g., the sperm whale: 75 minutes, the Weddell seal: 60 minutes). Water mammals that come ashore are very clumsy on land. The mammals pictured on the cubes are: **porpoise**, **elephant seal**, **sea lion**, **whale**, **manatee**, and **walrus**. {Find out a little bit more about each pictured animal. Roll the cubes. Have children make up their own animal. If the cubes show a seal and walrus, a child could name it sealrus: barks like a seal, walks like a walrus.}

Cheetah Flip Book (p. 13, **136**): The **cheetah** is the fastest running mammal (60 miles per hour) and can be found from Africa to Asia. It is a member of the cat family and, like other cats around the world, it has a rough tongue and sharp, cutting teeth for eating meat. Cats are carnivores. Unlike other cats, the cheetah has no retractable claws, thus making it the most unusual member of the cat family. Other members of the cat family include: lions, tigers, jaguars, panthers, and house cats. {Find out speeds of other animals including humans. Show your results on a line graph.}

Chipmunk Cup Puppet (p. 14, **135**): The **chipmunk** is a member of the rodent family. Rodents are the largest order of mammals. They live on every continent and in every type of environment from the arctic to the tropics. Most rodents eat plants, seeds, and nuts. Other rodents include mice, rats, squirrels, beavers, and porcupines.

Unusual Mammals Match and Sort Cards (pp. 15–16, **138**): These animals are all mammals, but they have some unusual characteristics. The **duck-billed platypus** and the **echidna** (or **spiny anteater**) are the only mammals that lay eggs. Mother platypuses and echidnas keep the eggs warm and feed their babies milk like other mammals. These animals can be found in Australia. The **kangaroo, koala,** and **opossum** also live in Australia. The mothers have pouches on their tummys in which their babies are born, nurtured, and carried. **Armadillos** are covered with bony plates except on their ears and legs. When they are born, armadillos have soft, leathery skin; the bony plates harden as they mature and become fully grown. Armadillos have no teeth, and catch insects with their long, sticky tongues. **Bats** are the only mammals that fly. Their forelimbs are wings that are very different from that of birds. Bats have poor eyesight, therefore depend on their keen sense of sound to find food. The **aardvark** has no teeth and eats ants and termites. {How are they the same? How are they different? Chart or graph results.}

Mammal Eating Habits

Plant Eating Mammals (Herbivores) with Hooves (Ungulates) Match and Sort Cards (pp. 17–18, **138**): These animals are mainly plant-eaters. Some are single-toed (solid hoof) like the horse or rhinoceros. Others are even-toed (split hoof) like the deer, cow, bison, and pig. Some have horns that they use for defense and mating. Horns are made of a material similar to that of human fingernails. Cattle, sheep, and goats have horns which continue to grow throughout their lives. Only the pronghorn sheds its horns. Other ungulates have antlers. Antlers are solid bony growths on male animals like the deer, elk, and moose. Their antlers are shed each year.

Meat-Eating Mammals (Carnivores) Picture Cubes (pp. 19–20, **140**): Most meat-eating mammals are predators. They have sharp teeth for cutting and tearing meat. Meat-eating mammals have feet that are padded with claws and live all over the world. They range in size from the tiny weasel to the giant bear.

Fox Hand Puppet (pp. 21–22, **137**): **Foxes** are kin to dogs and live all over the world. Many build dens underground for protection and for raising their young. Foxes are meat-eaters. {Use puppets to stage a play.}

Mammal Families

Mammal Homes Lift-and-Looks (pp. 23–26, **138**): Some mammals make homes for their young. **Beavers** live in lodges in the middle of lakes and streams. **Squirrels** build leafy nests high in trees. **Rabbits** burrow in underground homes called warrens. **Bears** live in caves where they hibernate and protect their babies.

Mammal Family Lace-Ups (pp. 27–29, **137**): Mammal adults and babies are often called by different names. Following is a list of some mammal names you can discuss with your class as they are stitching their lace-ups.

Mammal	Male	Female	Babies	Mammal	Male	Female	Babies
Bear	Boar	Sow	Cub	**Horse**	Stallion	Mare	Foal
Cat	Tom	Queen	Kitten	**Lion**	Lion	Lioness	Cub
Cattle	Bull	Cow	Calf	**Rabbit**	Buck	Doe	Bunny
Deer	Buck	Doe	Fawn	**Sheep**	Ram	Ewe	Lamb
Dog	Dog	Bitch	Pup	**Pig**	Boar	Sow	Piglet
Elephant	Bull	Cow	Calf	**Tiger**	Tiger	Tigress	Cub
Fox	Dog	Vixen	Kit	**Whale**	Bull	Cow	Calf

A Whale Is Born Mini-Book (p. 30, **139**): After assembling the book, read it to the class and discuss the pictures. Talk about how other mammals take care of their babies. Talk about how they communicate. Talk about how and what babies learn from their parents.

Chimpanzee Expressions Wheel (pp. 31–32, **136**): Mother **chimpanzees** "talk" to their young through emotions. It is their form of communication. Many mammals also "talk" by making sounds that attract mates, warn enemies to stay away, and protect their young. {Children can show how they express the same emotions as the chimpanzees. Talk about other emotions and how we express them with our faces and with our bodies.}

Big Book and Bulletin Board Mammals

Asian elephant

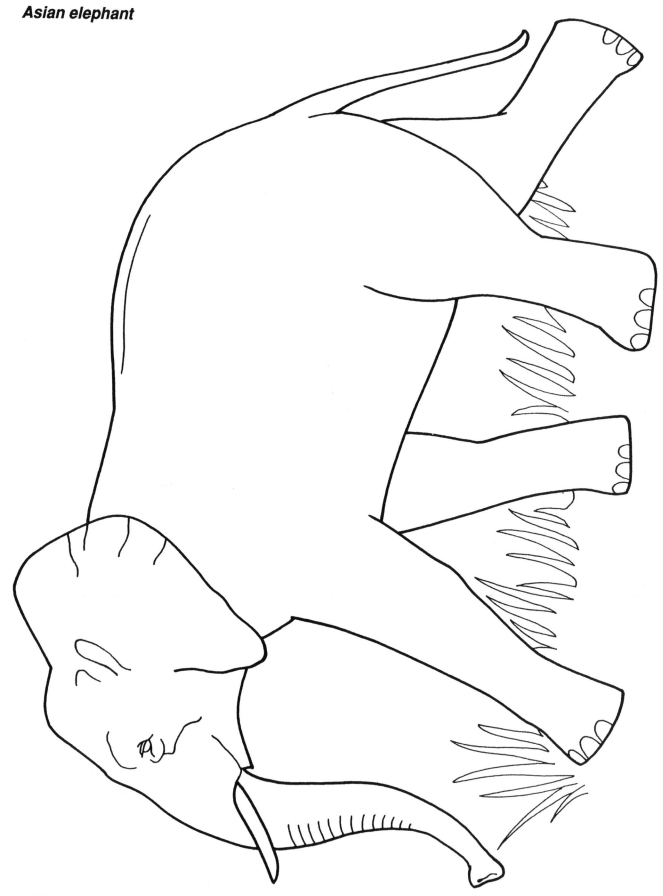

Big Book and Bulletin Board Mammals

beaver

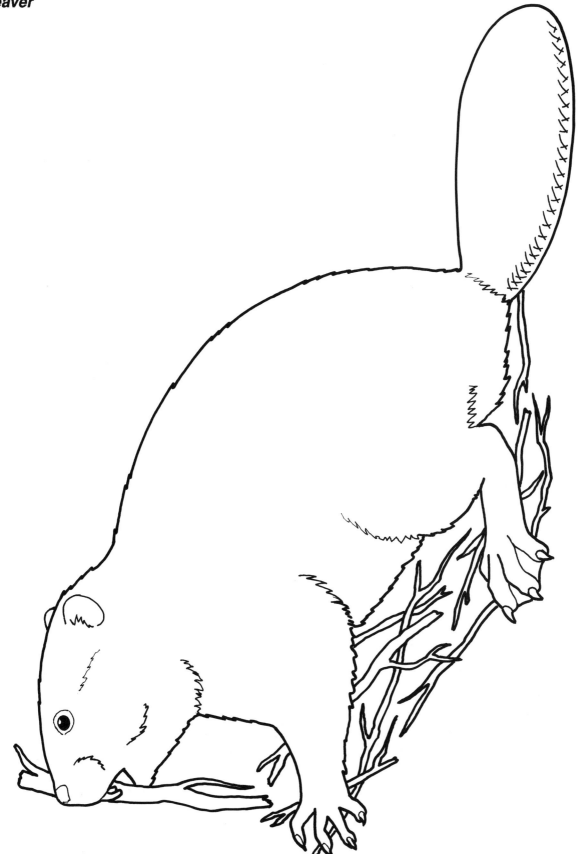

Big Book and Bulletin Board Mammals

people

Water Mammals Picture Cubes

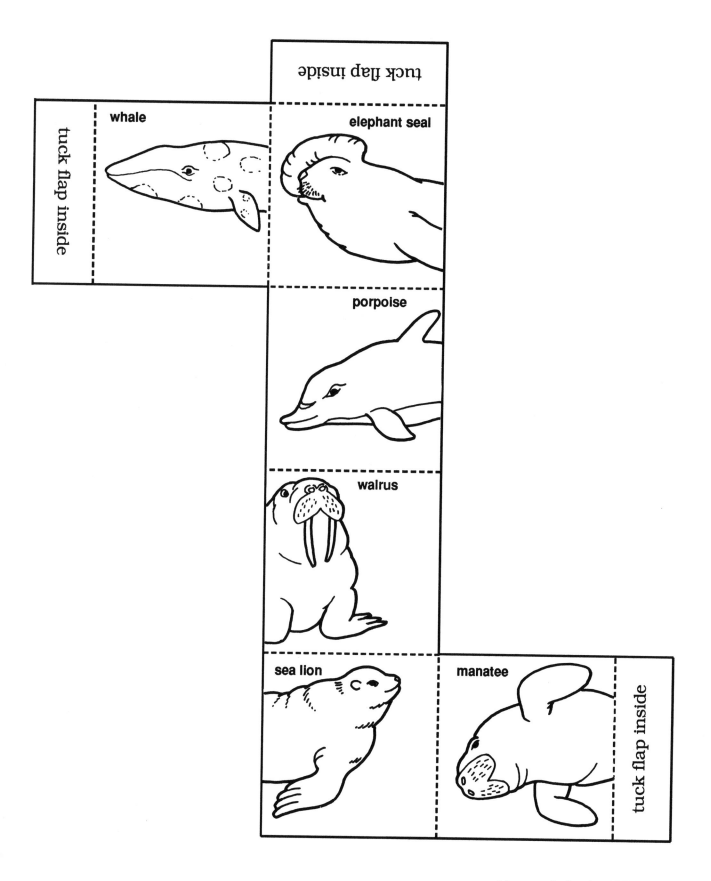

Water Mammals Picture Cube

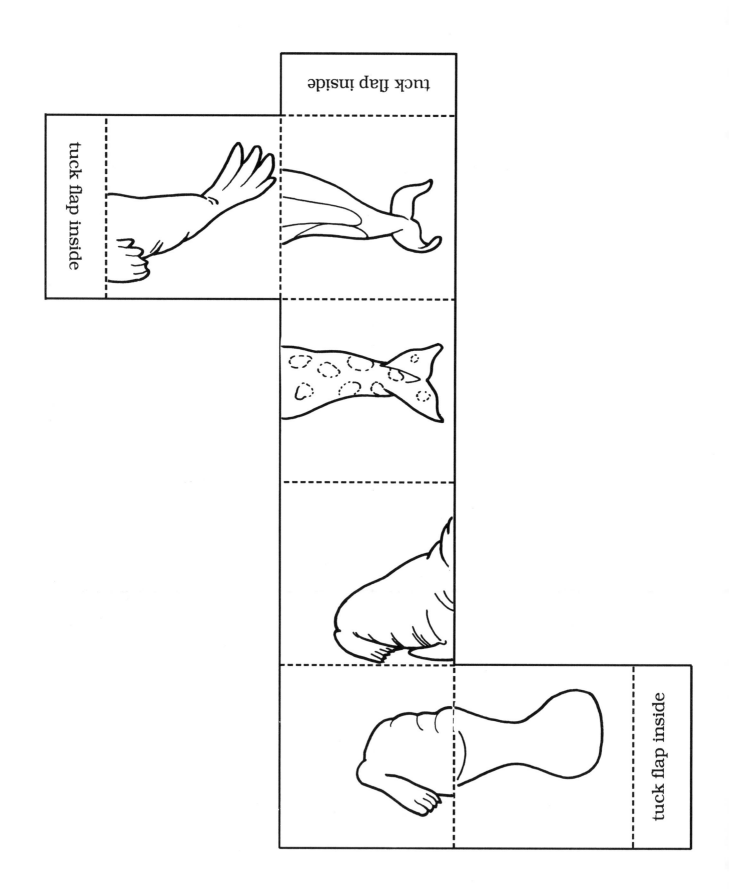

Cheetah Flip-Book

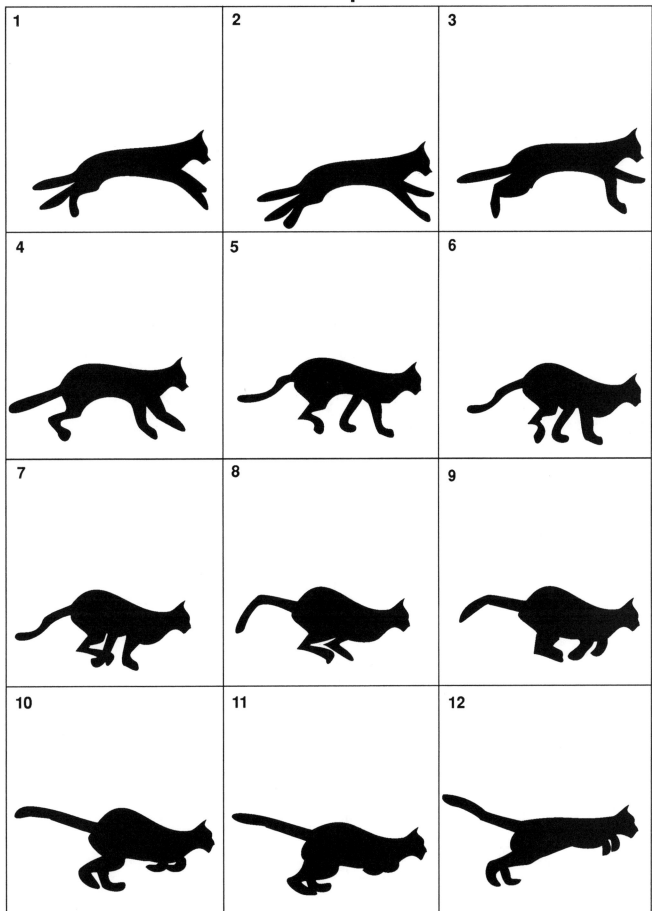

Chipmunk Cup Puppet

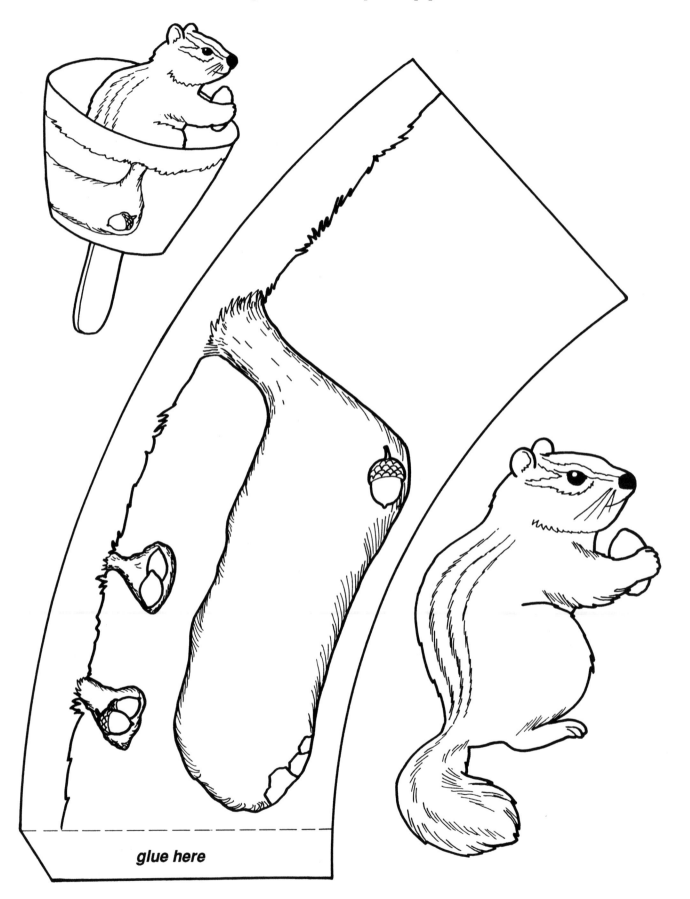

glue here

Unusual Mammals Match and Sort Cards

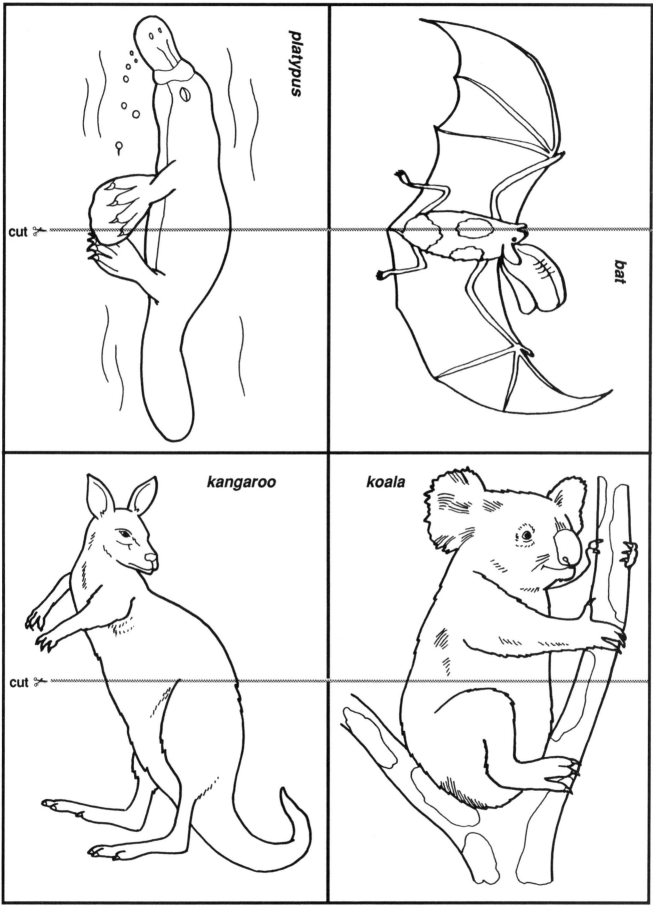

platypus

bat

cut ✂

kangaroo

koala

cut ✂

Unusual Mammals Match and Sort Cards

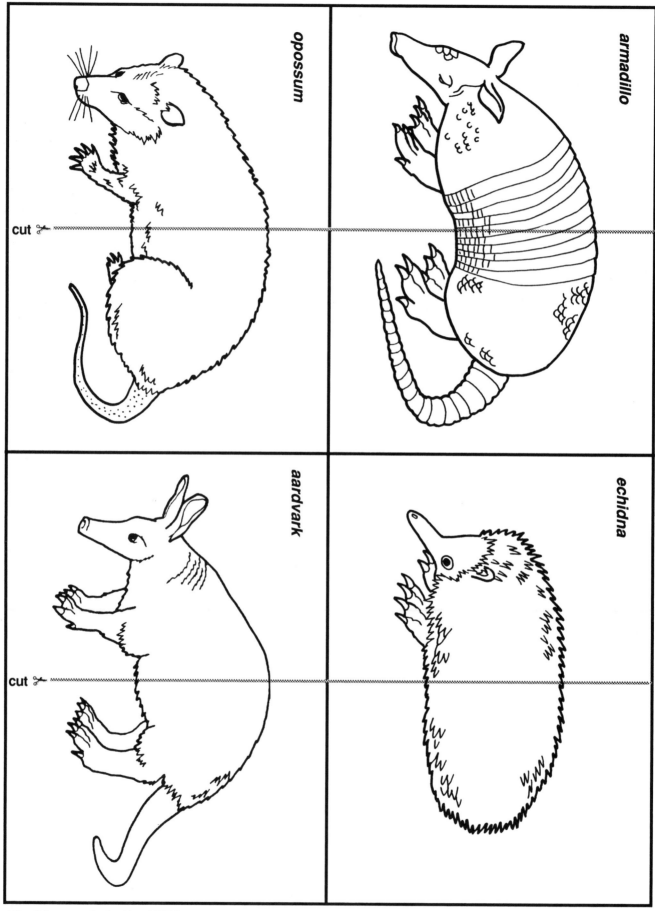

opossum

armadillo

aardvark

echidna

cut ✂

cut ✂

Mammals with Hooves Match and Sort Cards

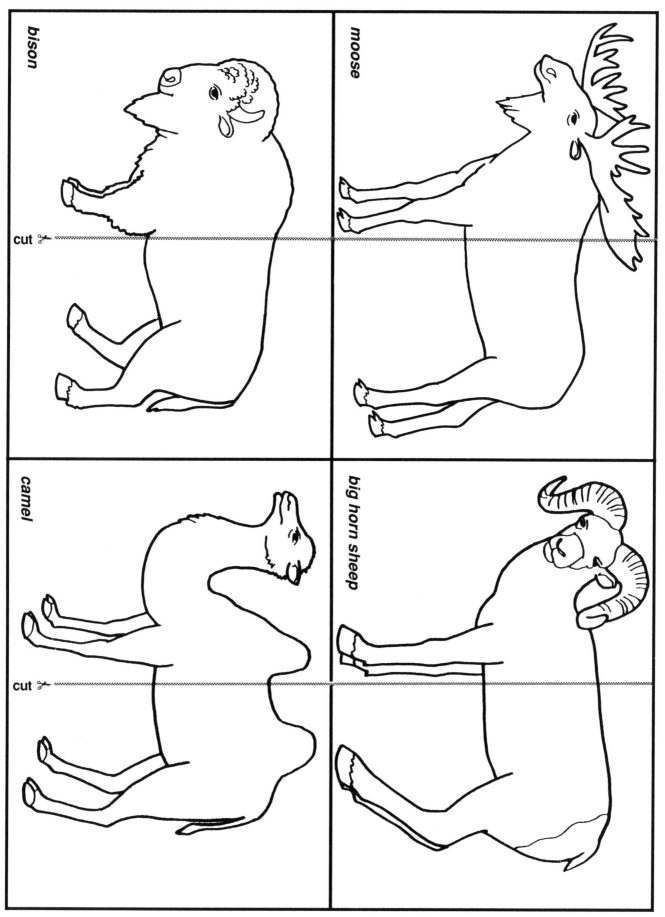

bison

moose

cut ✂

camel

big horn sheep

cut ✂

Mammals with Hooves Match and Sort Cards

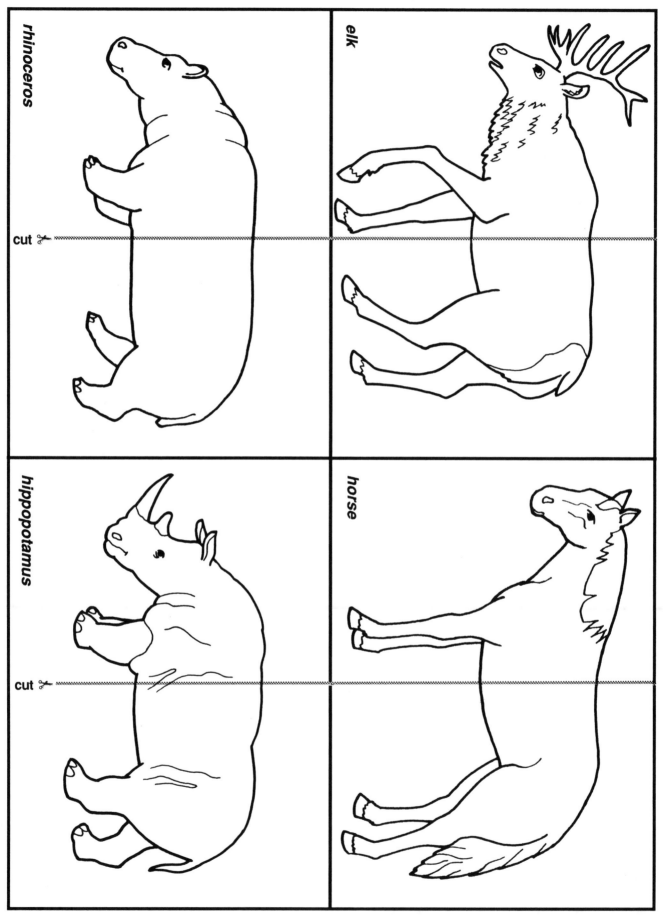

rhinoceros

elk

cut ✂

hippopotamus

horse

cut ✂

Meat-Eating Mammals Picture Cubes

Meat-Eating Mammals Picture Cubes

Fox Hand Puppet

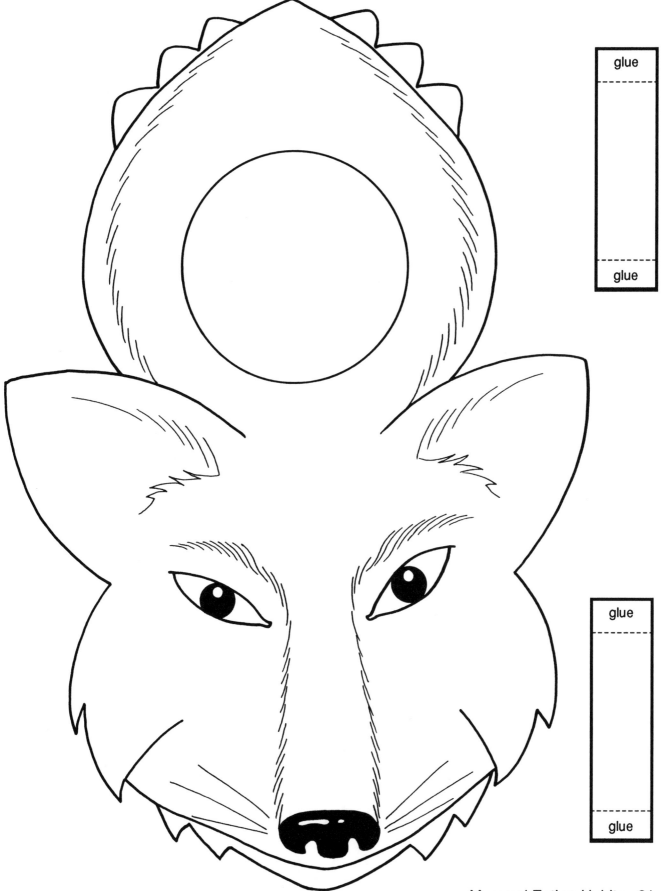

glue

glue

glue

glue

Fox Hand Puppet

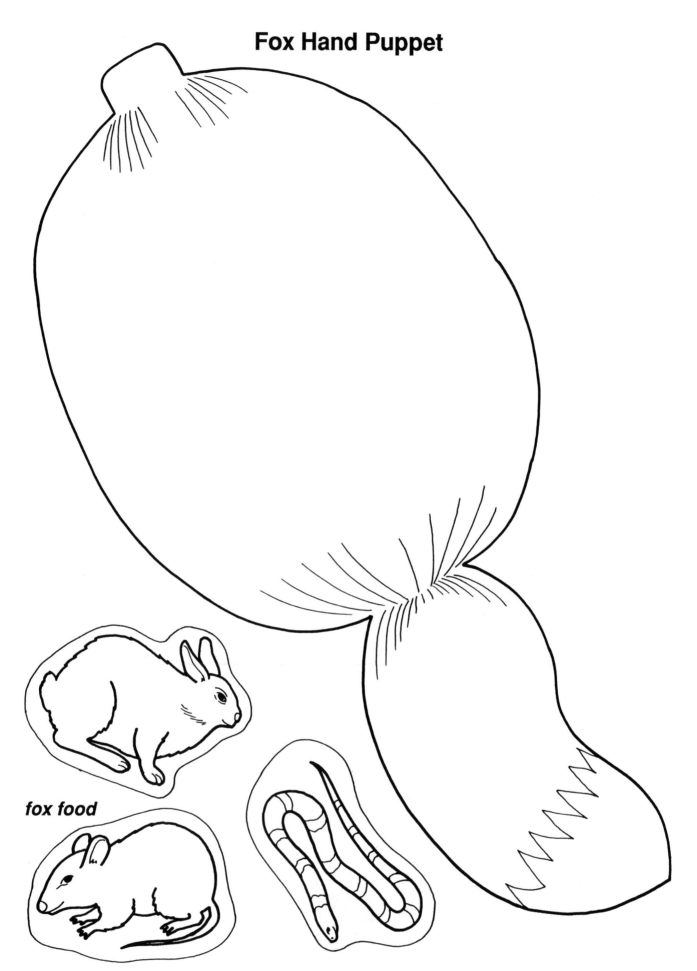

fox food

Mammal Homes Lift-and-Look

Mammal Homes Lift-and-Look

squirrel nest

beaver lodge

Mammal Homes Lift-and-Look

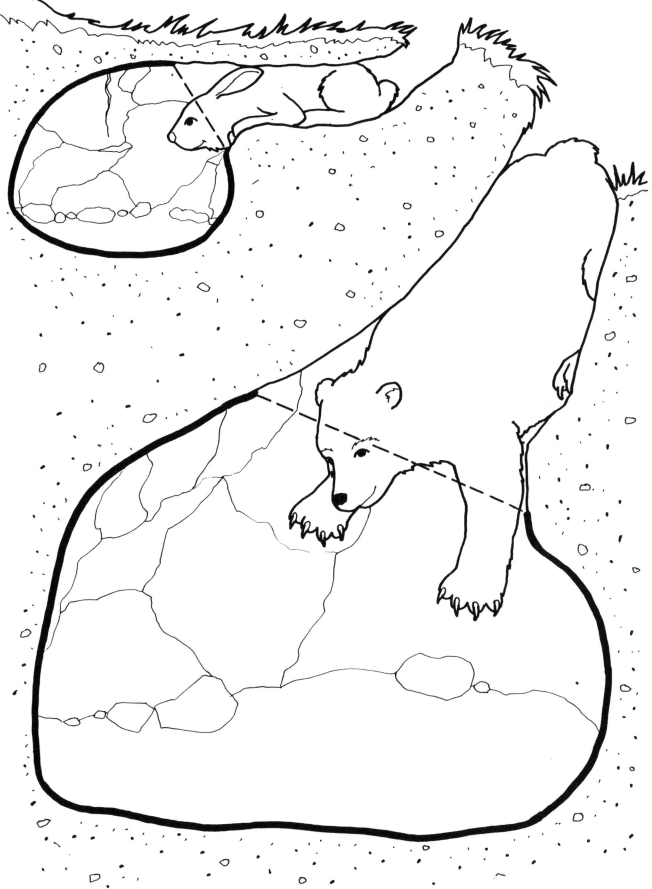

Mammal Homes Lift-and-Look

rabbit warren

bear den

Mammal Family Lace-Ups

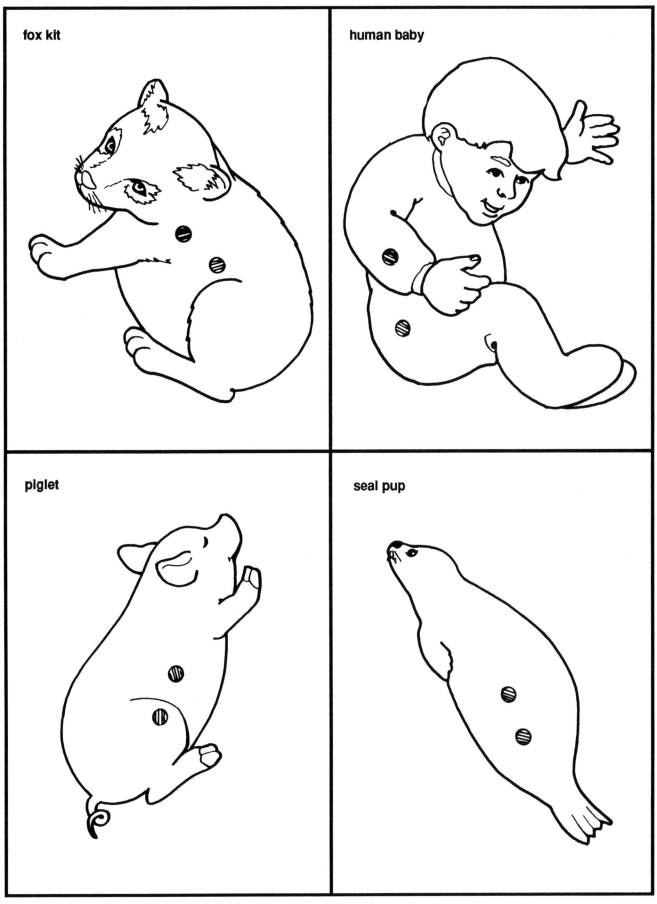

fox kit

human baby

piglet

seal pup

Mammal Family Lace-Ups

Mammal Family Lace-Ups

A Whale Is Born Mini-Book

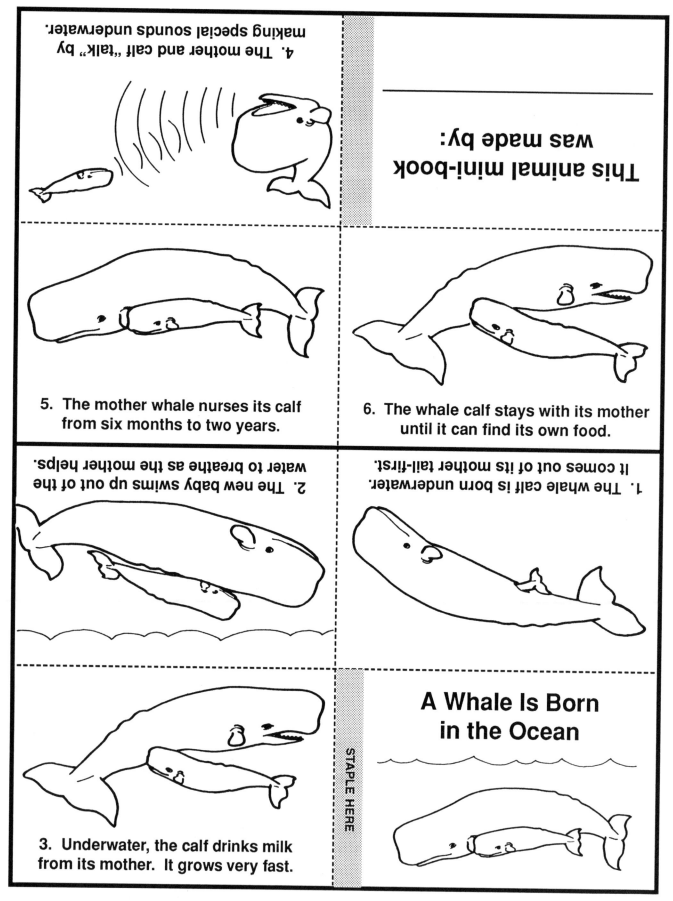

4. The mother and calf "talk" by making special sounds underwater.

This animal mini-book was made by:

_____

5. The mother whale nurses its calf from six months to two years.

6. The whale calf stays with its mother until it can find its own food.

2. The new baby swims up out of the water to breathe as the mother helps.

1. The whale calf is born underwater. It comes out of its mother tail-first.

3. Underwater, the calf drinks milk from its mother. It grows very fast.

A Whale Is Born in the Ocean

STAPLE HERE

Chimpanzee Expressions Wheel

cut
out

cut out

Chimpanzee Expressions Wheel

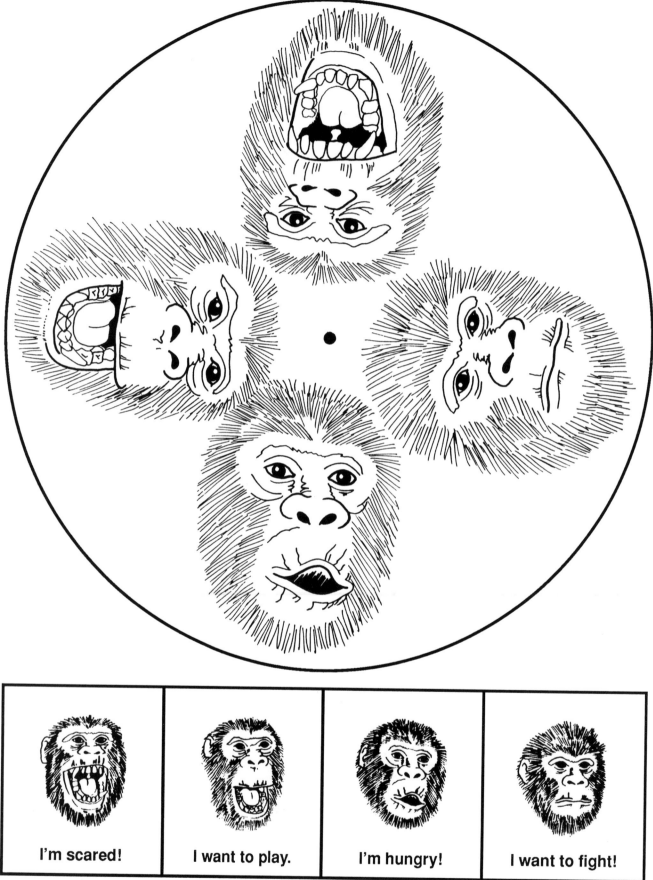

I'm scared!	I want to play.	I'm hungry!	I want to fight!

Chapter 2: AMPHIBIANS

Teacher: Use these facts with your class to stimulate discussion and to create big books, fact wheels, posters, and bulletin boards. Reproduce the facts chart below for children to use for reference.

What You Should Know About Amphibians
- Amphibians are the only animals that can live in water for part of their life and on land for another part.
- Amphibians breathe using their gills or lungs, and through their skin.
- Amphibians can not live in very cold climates.
- Amphibians live in or near water.
- Examples: frog, toad, salamander

Amphibians in the Wild
- Frogs have smooth, moist skin. They are slim with little eyes.
- Toads have bumpy, dry skin. They are fat with big eyes.
- Frogs jump and toads hop. Both have strong hind legs.
- Frogs and toads often shed their skin and eat it.
- Salamanders are long and skinny with a tail and four short legs. They are good runners.
- Amphibians can make many sounds. They call out to find a mate, to warn other amphibians, or to frighten enemies.

Amphibian Eating Habits
- Amphibians do not need to eat as often as warm-blooded animals.
- Adult amphibians eat insects and other small animals such as worms, turtles, mice, or insects.
- Frogs and toads have sticky tongues to help them catch flying insects. The tongue is attached to the front of the mouth, rather than the back.
- As tadpoles, frogs and toads eat plants.

Amphibian Families
- Amphibians lay jelly-covered eggs in water.
- Most amphibians do not take care of their eggs or their babies when they hatch.
- Amphibians do not look like small adults when they are born. They grow in a larval stage in water.
- Young amphibians are often called tadpoles.

Teacher Page

The numbers shown after the titles indicate pages where patterns and assembly directions (**bold**) are found.

What You Should Know About Amphibians

Big Book and Bulletin Board Amphibians (pp. 36–38, **134**): Use the pictures on these pages to start your study of amphibians. You may want to reduce or enlarge them to be more in proportion. The facts on the preceding page will guide you in your classroom discussions.

Amphibian Picture Cubes (pp. 39–40, **140**): **Toads** have bumpy skin and short legs for hopping, and **frogs** have smooth skin and long legs for leaping. **Salamanders** have long bodies and tails, and have four toes or less on their feet. {There are one pair of frogs, toads, and salamanders on the cubes. Help children note the differences among them. After children become familiar with the cubes, they may want to mix them up and invent new names for their "made-up" animals such as "toadamanders" or "froads."}

Amphibians in the Wild

Salamander Color-by-Number Puzzles (pp. 41–42, **135**): **Salamanders** avoid direct sun; they are *nocturnal* animals. During the breeding season they move about more and hence are more likely to be seen. Some spend their entire lives in water; others live on moist land, returning to water only to mate and lay eggs. {Fill in the name of the salamander on the line so that children will know which color chart to follow. Some children may need help drawing in spots and coloring.}

Amphibian Button Trails (pp. 43–45, **134**): Amphibians live in many places. Tree frogs live in trees above rivers or ponds. Toads live in grassy areas. They can often be found in parks and backyards. Salamanders live under leaves. They hide there until night when they come out to find food. {Children may need help cutting the trails, but they will enjoy moving the animals around the trails to their homes. The class may want to write a story, poem, or song to tell about a tree frog going from a pond to a tree.}

Amphibians in Spring Lift-and-Look (pp. 46–47, **138**): When the weather gets warm, amphibians wake from their winter naps which is known as *hibernation*. They find mates and breed. The female then lays eggs in shallow water.

Amphibians in Winter Lift-and-Look (pp. 48–49, **138**): Amphibians are cold-blooded. When the weather is cold, amphibians go to sleep for months at a time. Some bury themselves underground or in muddy ponds. Salamanders cover themselves with layers of leaves in woody areas.

Toad Cup Puppet (p. 50, **135**): Toads live on land. They don't have to be near water all the time like frogs. When frightened they hop under leaves or rocks to get away from their enemies. Some can also blow up their bodies to look bigger to scare their enemies.

Amphibian Eating Habits

Frog Mask (p. 51, **138**): Many frogs have long, sticky tongues that help them quickly snatch insects into their mouths. Frogs and toads have different chirps and squeaks for when captured or breeding, or to announce the coming of rain. {Using the masks, children may pretend to be frogs and act out their favorite scene from any "frog" book.}

Salamanders at Night Lace-Up (p. 52, **137**): Many scientists believe there are more salamanders in woody areas than mammals and birds. They are seldom seen because they hide under leaves during the day. They come out at night to find food. Worms, insects, and small water animals are favorite foods.

Skink Hand Puppet (pp. 53–54, **137**): Skinks look like small salamanders. They eat insects and worms.

Amphibian Families

A Frog Grows Up Pop-Up Card (p. 55, **141**): **Tadpoles** are the immature or larval stage of frogs and toads. As tadpoles hatch and begin to grow, they feed on microscopic plants and spend all of their time in water. They breathe by means of gills. When they grow into adults, they breathe with lungs and many live on land near water.

From Egg to Tadpole to Frog Mini-Book (p. 56, **139**): This book goes through the life cycle of amphibians in more detail. After the book is assembled, read it to the class. Talk about the pictures. Most amphibians do not take care of their young. A few do, however.

Big Book and Bulletin Board Amphibians

red-backed salamander

Big Book and Bulletin Board Amphibians

bull frog

Big Book and Bulletin Board Amphibians

Sonoran desert toad

Amphibian Picture Cubes

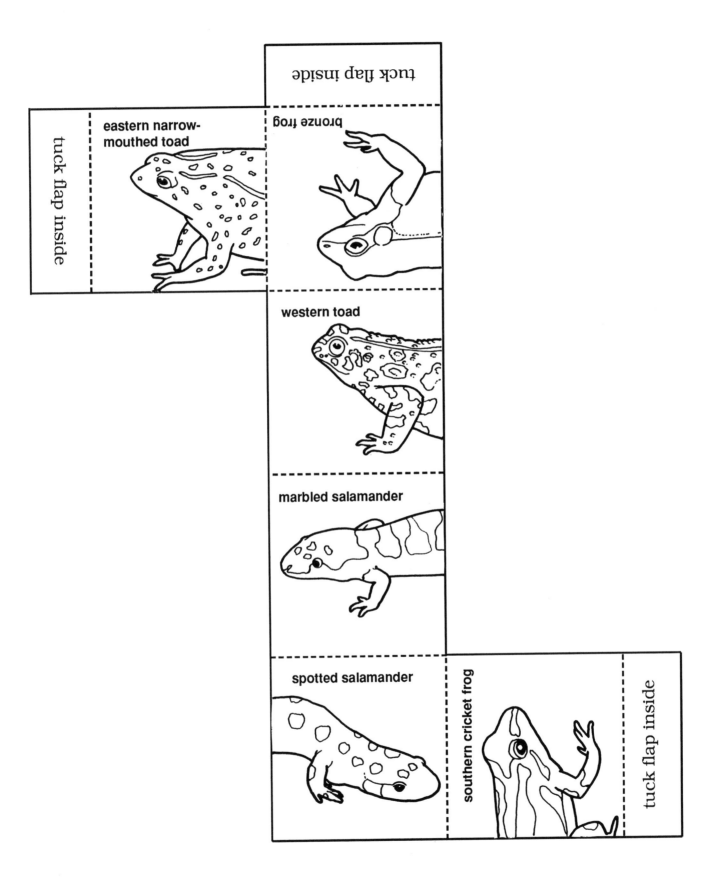

eastern narrow-mouthed toad

tuck flap inside

bronze frog

tuck flap inside

western toad

marbled salamander

spotted salamander

southern cricket frog

tuck flap inside

Amphibian Picture Cubes

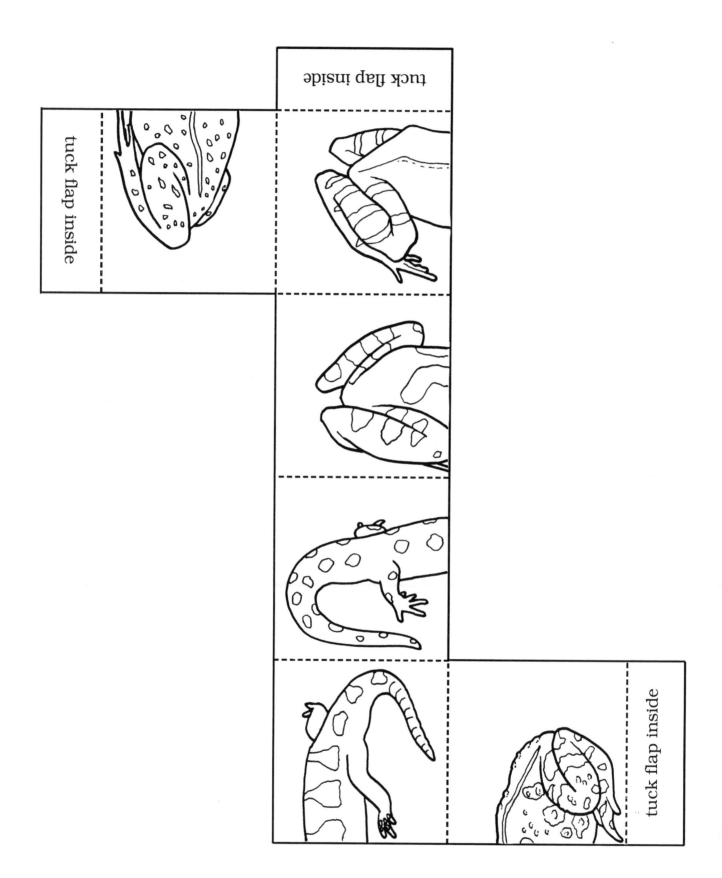

Salamander Color-by-Number Puzzle

salamander

Salamander Color-by-Number Puzzle

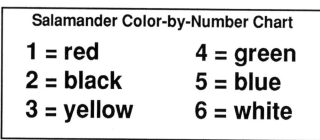

Salamander Color-by-Number Chart

1 = red	**4 = green**
2 = black	**5 = blue**
3 = yellow	**6 = white**

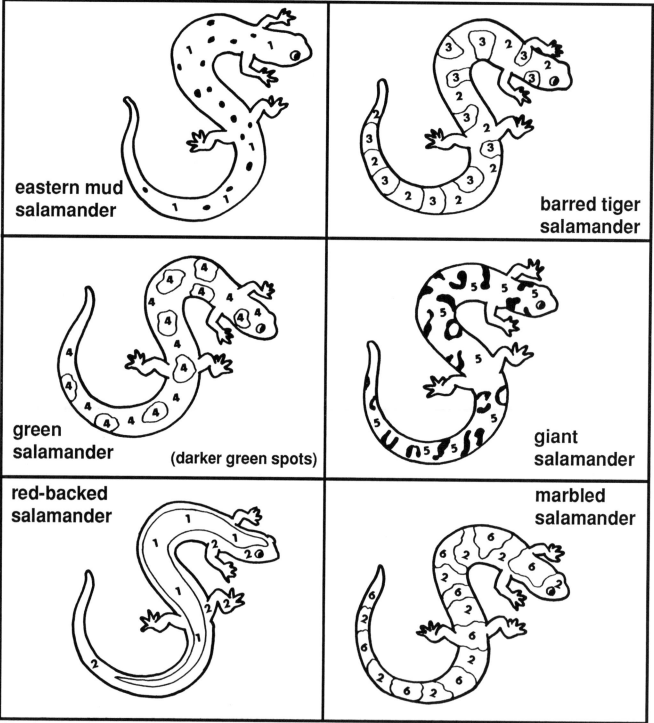

eastern mud
salamander

barred tiger
salamander

green
salamander

(darker green spots)

giant
salamander

red-backed
salamander

marbled
salamander

Tree Frog Button Trail

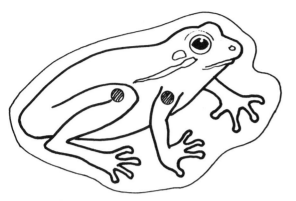

tree frog

To Make:

Toad Button Trail

To Make:

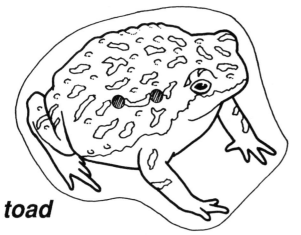

toad

Salamander Button Trail

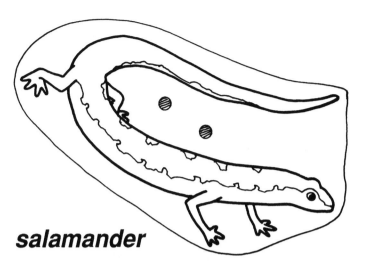

salamander

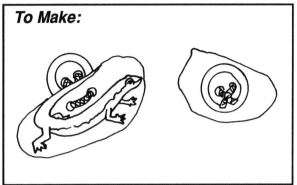

To Make:

Amphibians in Spring Lift-and-Look

Amphibians in Spring Lift-and-Look

salamanders

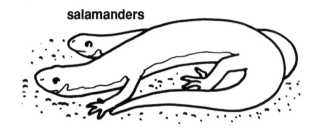

toad

frog

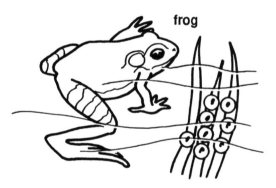

salamander

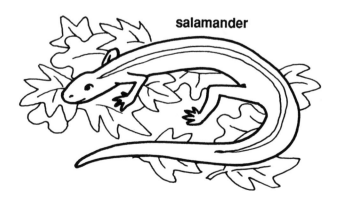

Amphibians in Winter Lift-and-Look

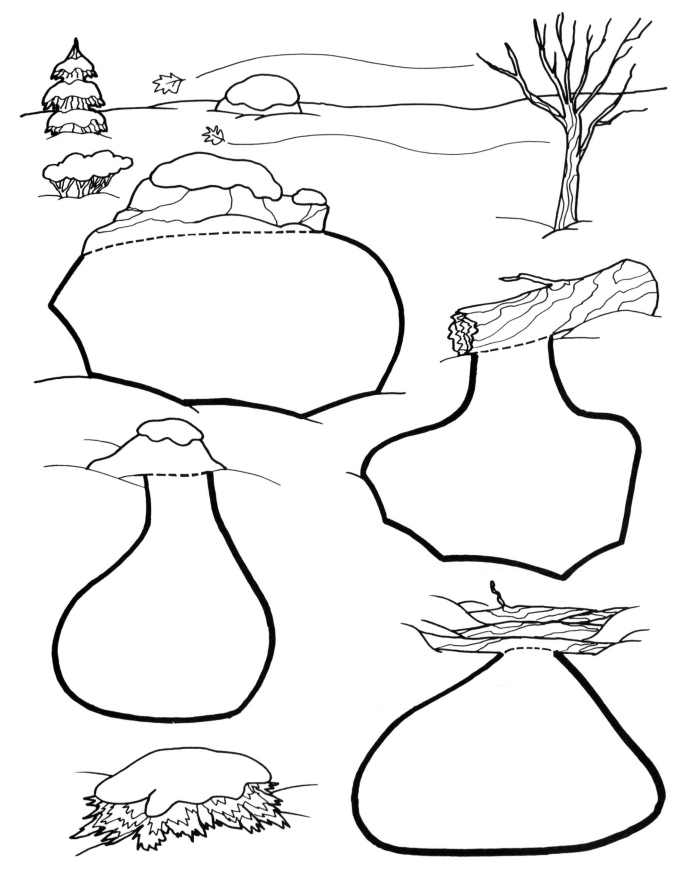

Amphibians in Winter Lift and Look

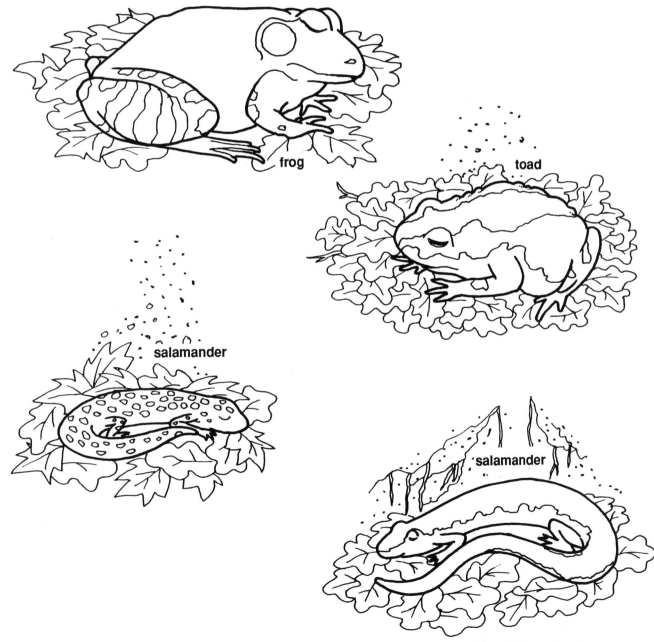

frog

toad

salamander

salamander

Toad Cup Puppet

glue here

Frog Mask

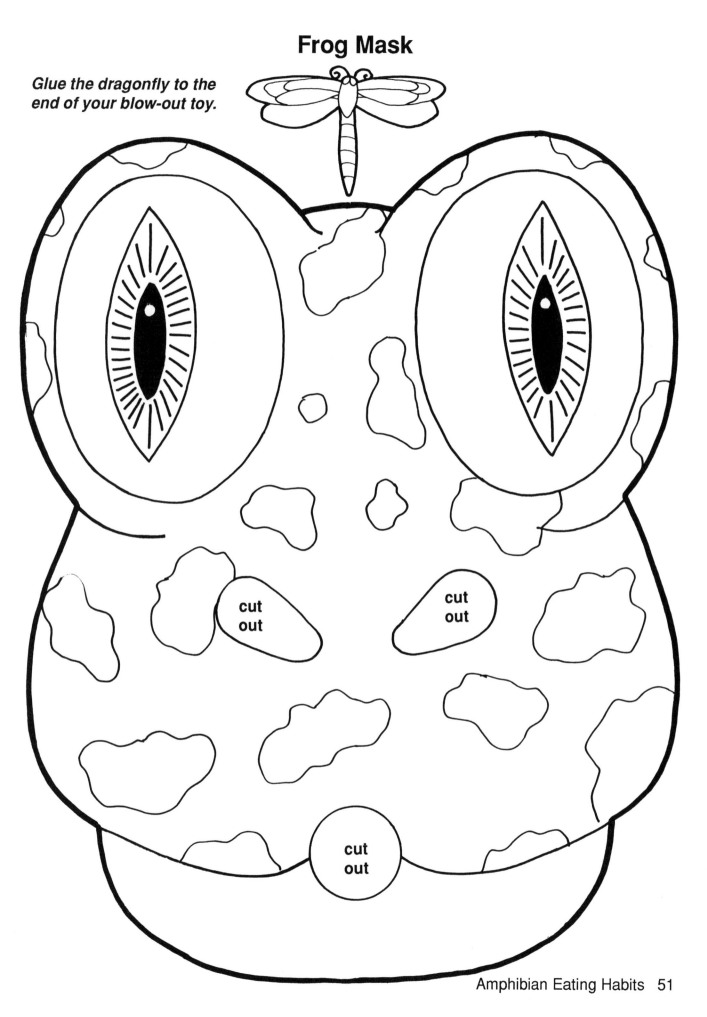

Glue the dragonfly to the end of your blow-out toy.

cut out

cut out

cut out

Salamanders at Night Lace-Up

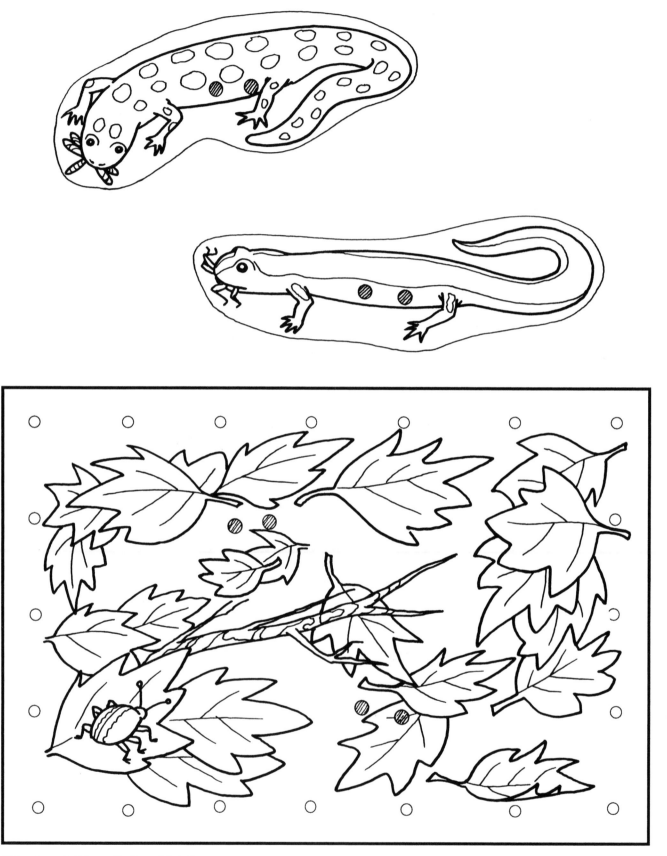

Mud Puppy Hand Puppet

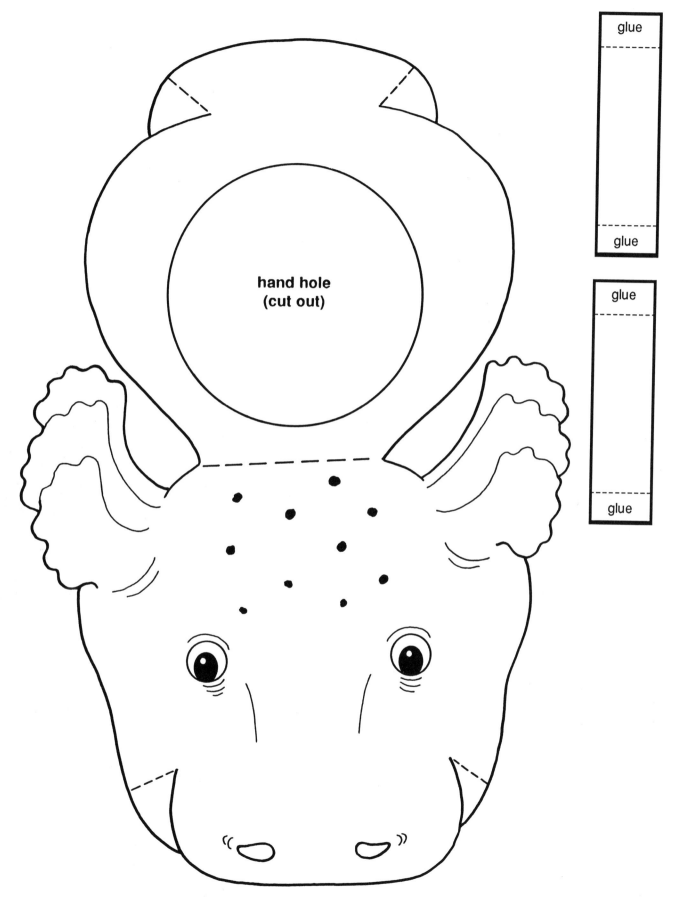

glue

glue

glue

glue

**hand hole
(cut out)**

Mud Puppy Hand Puppet

mud puppy food

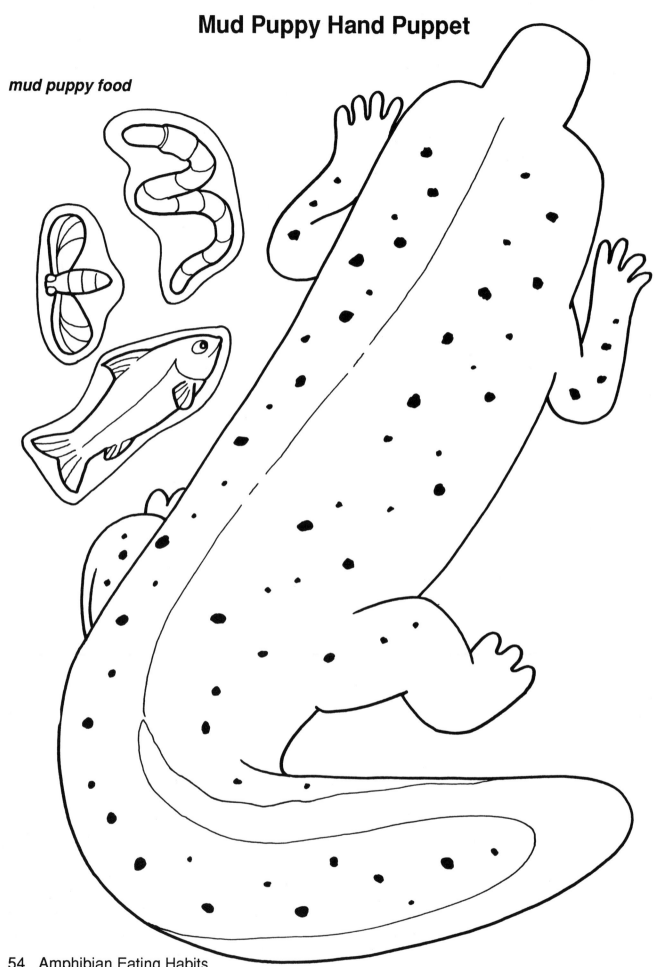

A Frog Grows Up Pop-Up Card

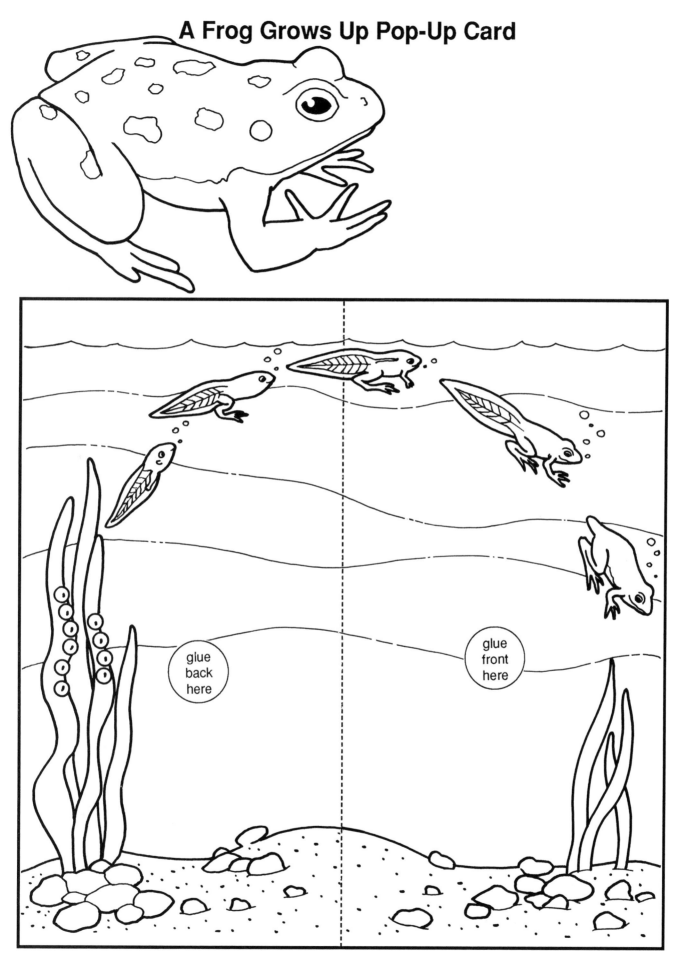

glue
back
here

glue
front
here

From Egg to Tadpole to Frog Mini-Book

4. Front legs and back legs grow. The tail shrinks.

This animal mini-book was made by:

_____

5. The mouth gets bigger. Lungs grow inside the body.

6. The tadpole has grown into a frog. It leaves the water to live on land.

2. The eggs are covered with clear "jelly." The eggs hatch in water.

1. A female frog lays many dozens of eggs in shallow water.

3. Tadpoles move their tails to swim. They eat plants. They breathe with gills.

STAPLE HERE

From Egg to Tadpole to Frog

Chapter 3: REPTILES

Teacher: Use these facts with your class to stimulate discussion and to create big books, fact wheels, posters, and bulletin boards. Reproduce the facts chart below for children to use for reference.

What You Should Know About Reptiles
- Reptiles have scaly, dry skin.
- Reptiles breathe with lungs.
- Reptiles are cold-blooded. Their temperature is the same as the environment.
- Most reptiles have claws on their feet.
- Some reptiles have teeth (alligator, crocodile).
- Examples: turtle, lizard, snake, crocodile

Reptiles in the Wild
- Reptiles can not live and be active in very cold climates.
- Reptiles live in many environments. Some live in woodlands (box turtle, garter snake, anole lizard)
- Others live in deserts (desert tortoise, monitor lizard, king snake, iguana).
- Others live in oceans and rivers (green sea turtle, mud turtle, mud snake).
- Reptiles hibernate in very cold weather. They sleep underground or buried in mud underwater.
- Most reptiles shed their skin as they grow.
- A turtle's body is enclosed in a shell. It is connected at the sides. There are openings for the legs, head, and tail.
- Tortoises are turtles that live on land.

Reptile Eating Habits
- Reptiles do not need to eat as often as warm-blooded animals.
- Reptiles are mostly meat-eaters. Some lizards eat plants (iguana).
- Some turtles eat plants (tortoise). Others eat animals (map turtle, snapping turtle). Some eat both (box turtle).
- Turtles have no teeth. The edges of the jaws are sharp.

Reptile Families
- Most female reptiles lay leathery eggs on land. Some give birth to live young.
- Reptiles look like small adults when they hatch or are born from their mothers.
- Most reptiles do not take care of their eggs or their babies when they hatch.

Teacher Page

The numbers shown after the titles indicate pages where patterns and assembly directions (**bold**) are found.

What You Should Know About Reptiles

Big Book and Bulletin Board Reptiles (pp. 60–62, **134**): Use the pictures on these pages to start your study of reptiles. You may want to reduce or enlarge them to be more in proportion. The facts on the preceding page will help you guide classroom discussions.

Reptiles Match and Sort Cards (pp. 63–64, **138**): Reptiles are found in different parts of the world, but are more plentiful in warmer climates. They are not always easy to find. Many are nocturnal and most are protectively colored. Three types of reptiles are shown on the cards. **Snakes** have no legs. **Lizards** have four legs. **Turtles** have shells. {To help children sort the cards into different types of reptiles, reproduce the chart below. Children cut out the match and sort cards and place them under the correct headings.}

SNAKES	LIZARDS	TURTLES

Reptiles in the Wild

Reptiles Picture Cubes (pp. 65–66, **140**): **Box turtles** live on land near water. They eat insects and berries. The **alligator** is the largest reptile (6–19 feet) in North America. During mating season its roar can be heard from a great distance. The **corn snake** often lives in corn fields. At night it hunts mice, birds, and bats. The **slider turtle's** *carapace* (upper shell) is rather flat with a notched edge on the rear. It lives in quiet waters of rivers and ponds. The **garter snake**, related to water snakes, is common all over North America. It ejects a smelly fluid from vent glands when captured. **Horned lizards** are found only in Canada, western United States, and Mexico. They live in the desert where they lie on rocks or half buried in sand. They capture insects with a quick snap of the tongue.

Turtle Peek-a-Boo Facts (pp. 67–68, **140**): Turtles appeared 200 million years ago, long before dinosaurs. Today they are found in almost every environment. {Reproduce the peek-a-boo on oak tag. Glue the shell to the body. Glue the facts under the appropriate illustration. Read the facts together.}

Snake Color-by-Number Mobiles (pp. 69–71, **135**): Snakes have many different colors and markings. Some live in trees. Others live on land or in water. Snakes can climb or move over almost any surface.

Tuatara Color-by-Number Puzzle (p. 72, **135**): Not many people know about these unusual reptiles. Tuataras date back millions of years. They lived during the time of the first dinosaurs. Tuatara eggs take about 15 months to hatch, longer than any other reptile. Some of them live over one hundred years. They are found only in New Zealand.

Reptiles in Summer Lift-and-Look (pp. 73–74 **138**): Reptiles are active in warm weather. They like to sun themselves on rocks or in warm water. All reptiles are cold-blooded. Their body temperature is always about the same as the air around them. Reptiles do not have to eat as much as mammals or birds. Some only eat several times a year. {After children have put together the lift-and-look, talk about what is happening in the pictures. How are reptiles active in summer?}

Reptiles in Winter Lift-and-Look (pp. 75–76, **138**): Reptiles are not active in cold weather. They hibernate underground or under rocks, or in mud underwater. When they hibernate, they go into a very deep sleep. They do not eat or drink. Their hearts beat much slower. They do not wake up until the weather is warm again. {Discuss hibernation after the lift-and-look is done. Lift the pictures to see the sleeping reptiles.}

Lizard Cup Puppet (p. 77, **135**): Most lizards are fast runners. They dart away from danger and enemies. Some lizards' tails snap off when an enemy grabs it. They run away and later grow a new tail. {When the cup puppet is finished, children can help the lizard hide.}

Reptile Eating Habits

Snapping Turtle Hand Puppet (pp. 78–79, **137**): Turtles have no teeth. They have horny beaks to rip up their food. They also use their claws to tear their food apart. They eat many foods like insects, fruit, worms, and mushrooms. {When the puppet is complete, children can "feed" their own snapping turtles.}

Reptile Families

Sea Turtle Mini-Book (p. 80, **139**): This book tells the story of a sea turtle. The female comes ashore only to lay eggs. Males never come ashore after they hatch. The tiny turtles make their way to the water as soon as they are hatched. Many of them don't make it. They are eaten by birds and other animals on the beach. Some are run over by cars. Cars are not allowed in many areas where sea turtles hatch. This is one way for us to protect these tiny babies.

Alligator Grows Up Pop-Up Card (p. 81, **141**): Alligators spend most of their time in water. Alligators are a little different from other reptiles when it comes to caring for their babies. Some of them guard the nest after they lay their eggs. The nests are made of mud and decaying plants that keep the eggs warm until they hatch. The adult alligators leave the nest after the young hatch.

Reptile Parent and Baby Wheel (p. 82, **136**): This wheel is very simple to use. It emphasizes that baby reptiles look like tiny adults when they hatch. This will help children see how reptiles are different from amphibians.

Big Book and Bulletin Board Reptiles

crocodile

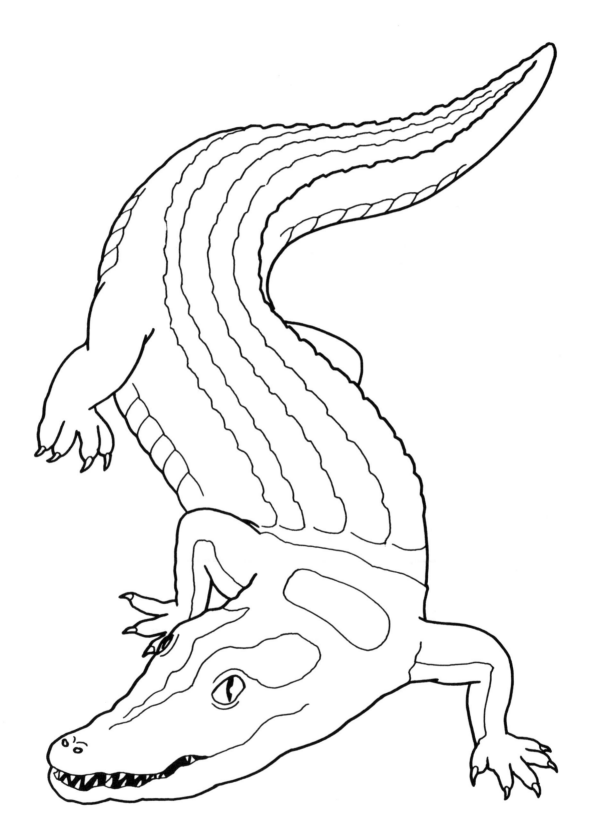

Big Book and Bulletin Board Reptiles

snapping turtle

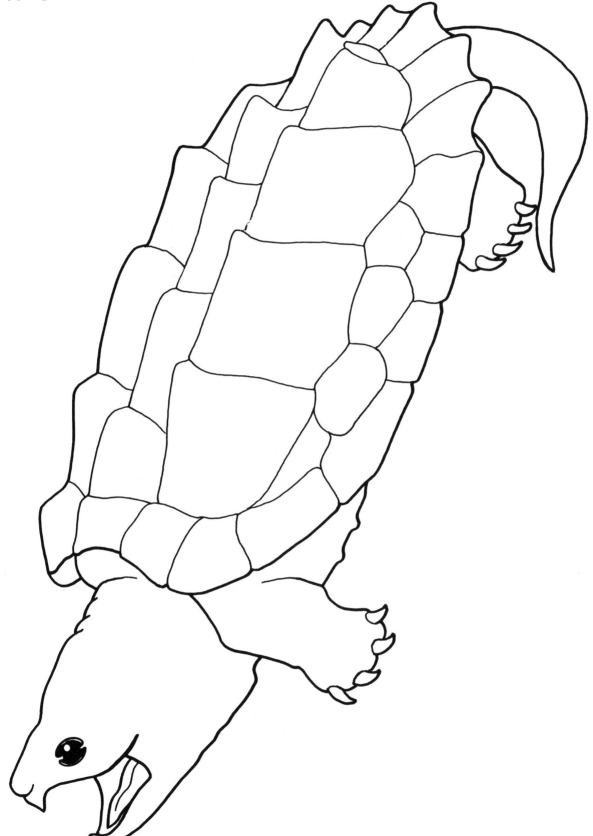

Big Book and Bulletin Board Reptiles

gila monster lizard

Reptile Match and Sort Cards

Reptile Match and Sort Cards

Reptile Picture Cubes

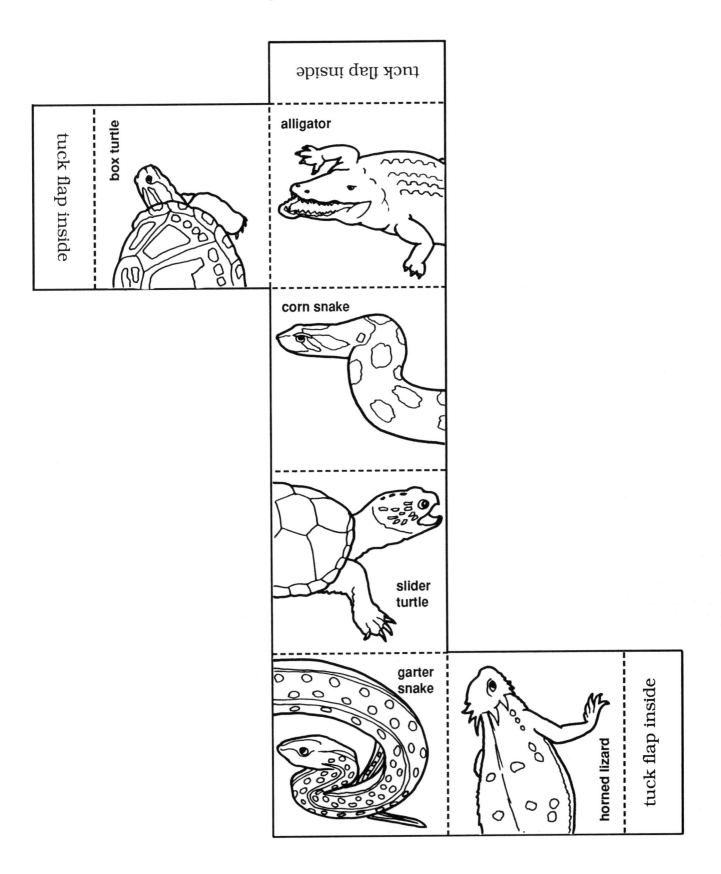

tuck flap inside

box turtle

tuck flap inside

alligator

corn snake

slider turtle

garter snake

horned lizard

tuck flap inside

Reptile Picture Cubes

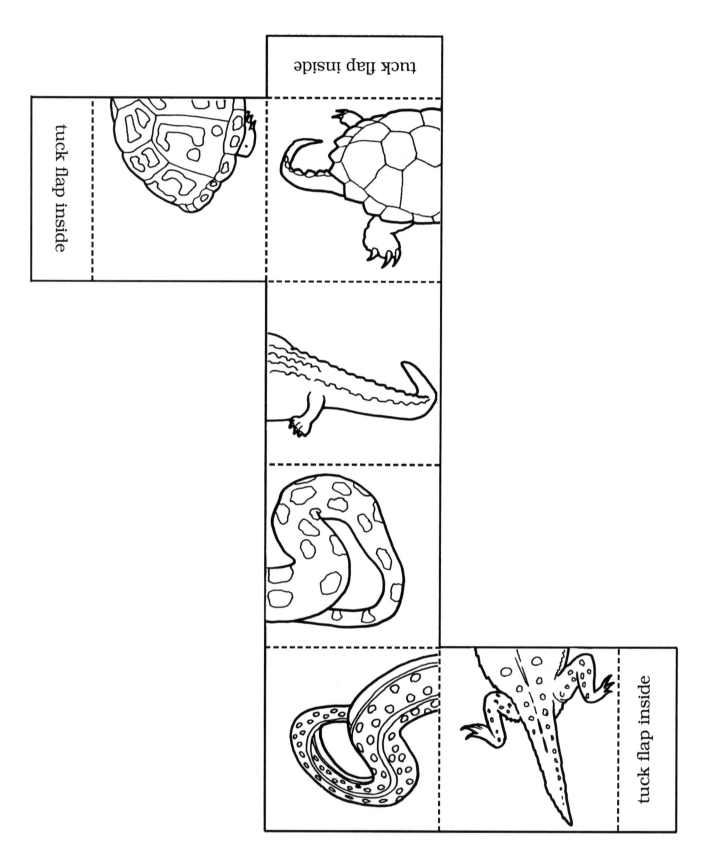

Turtle Peek-a-Boo Facts

Turtle Shell (Top)

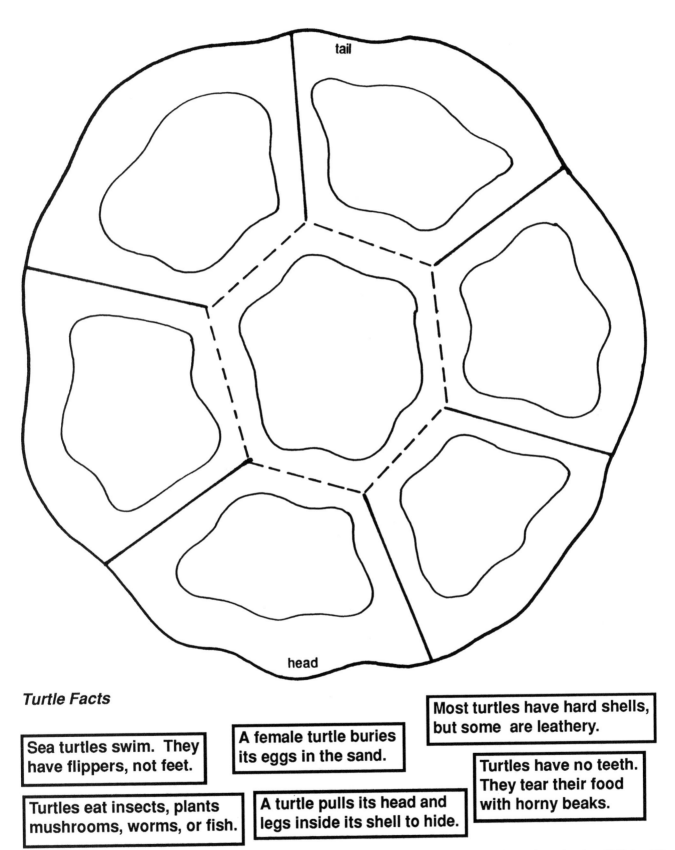

Turtle Facts

Sea turtles swim. They have flippers, not feet.

A female turtle buries its eggs in the sand.

Most turtles have hard shells, but some are leathery.

Turtles eat insects, plants mushrooms, worms, or fish.

A turtle pulls its head and legs inside its shell to hide.

Turtles have no teeth. They tear their food with horny beaks.

Turtle Peek-a-Boo Facts

Turtle Body (Bottom)

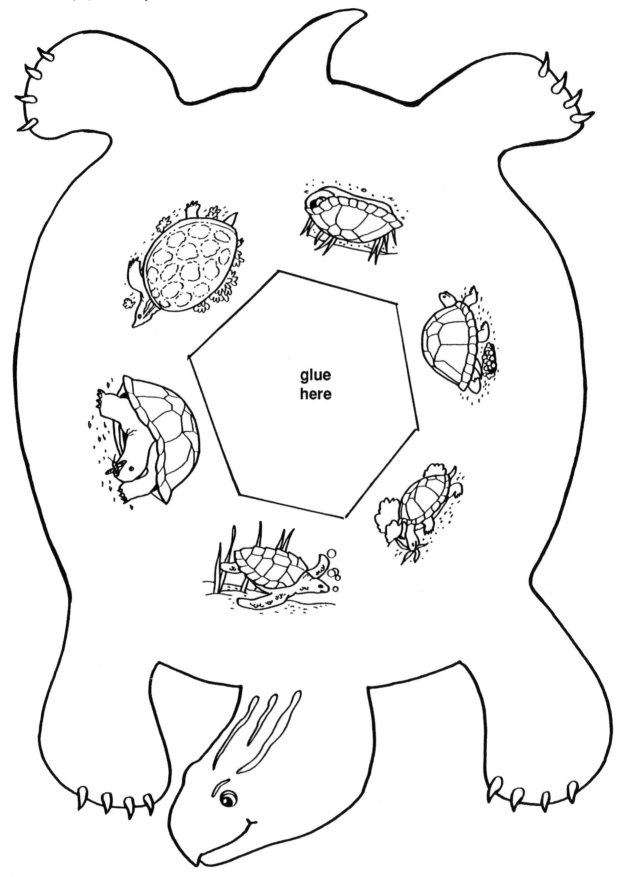

glue here

Color-by-Number Snake Mobile

Snake Mobile

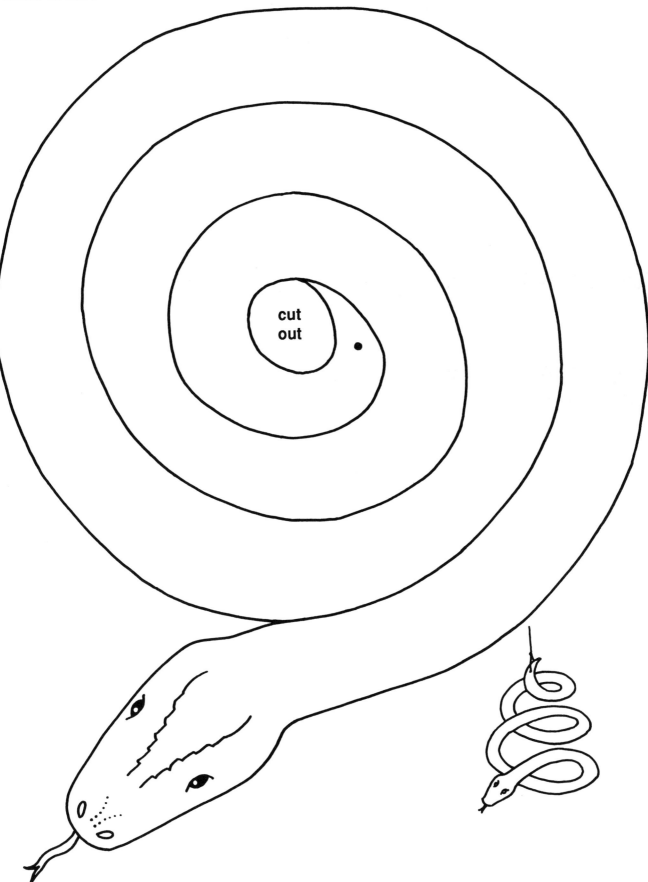

cut
out

Color-by-Number Snake Mobile

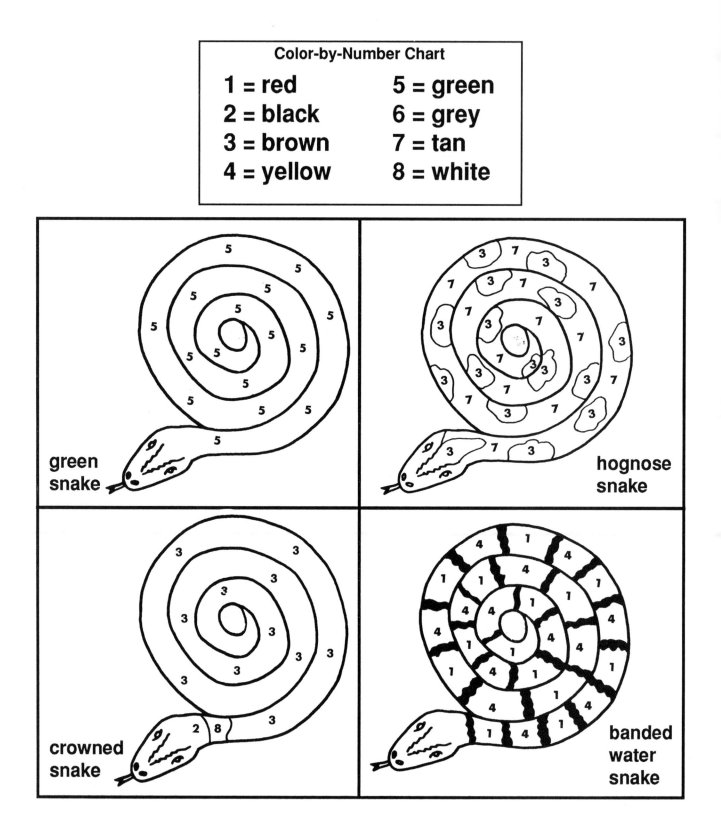

Color-by-Number Chart

1 = red   5 = green
2 = black   6 = grey
3 = brown   7 = tan
4 = yellow   8 = white

green snake

hognose snake

crowned snake

banded water snake

Color-by-Number Snake Mobile

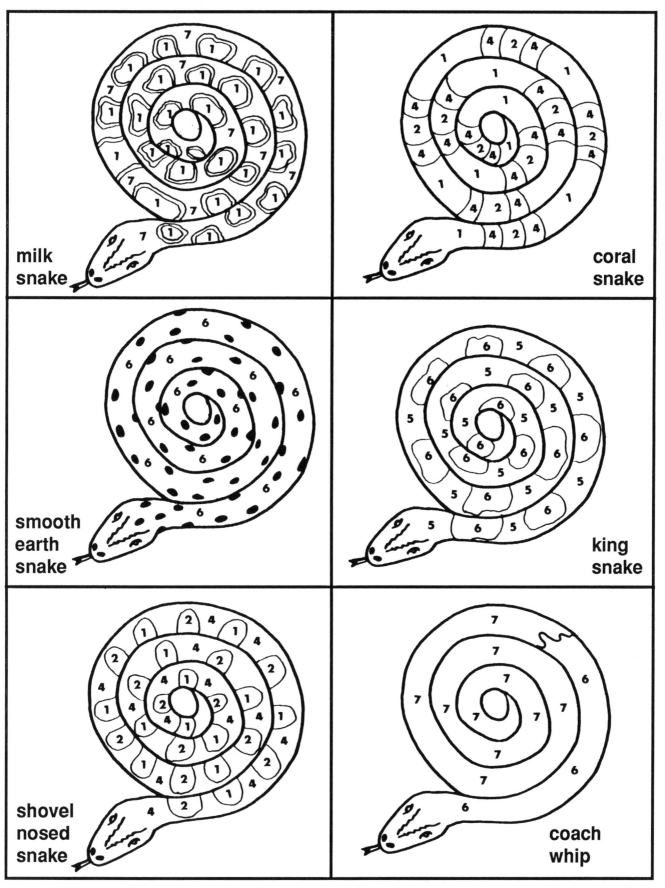

milk snake

coral snake

smooth earth snake

king snake

shovel nosed snake

coach whip

Tuatara Puzzle

Reptiles in Summer Lift-and-Look

Reptiles in Winter Lift-and-Look

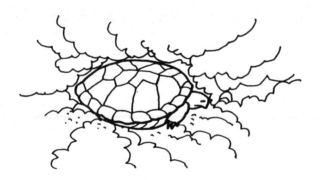

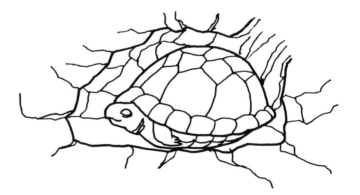

Lizard Cup Puppet

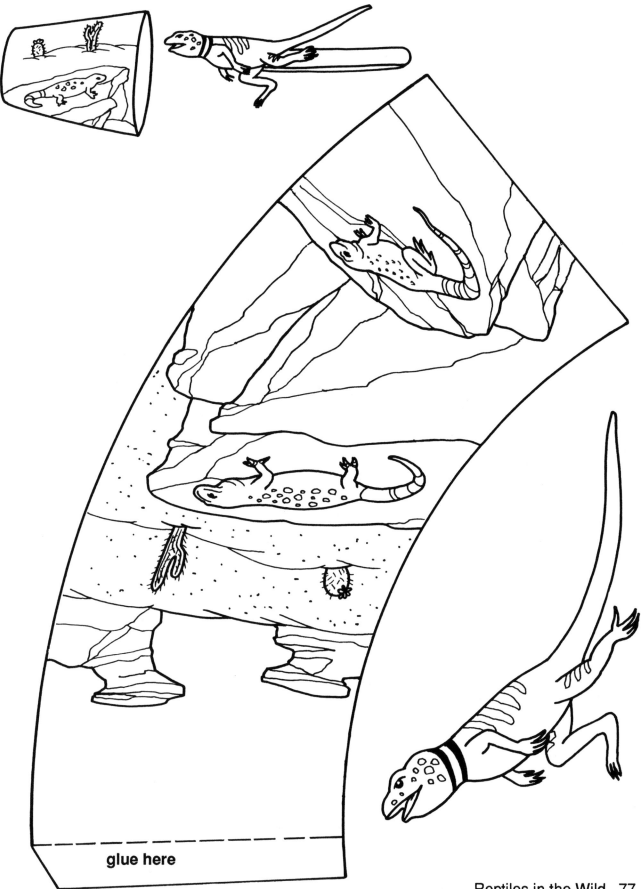

glue here

Snapping Turtle Hand Puppet

Snapping Turtle Shell

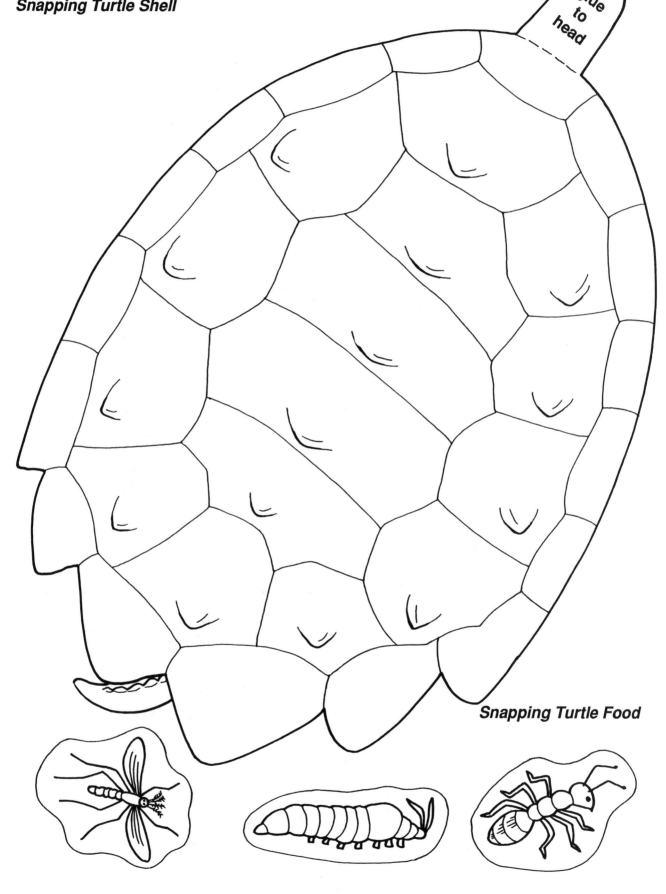

glue to head

Snapping Turtle Food

Snapping Turtle Hand Puppet

Snapping Turtle Head

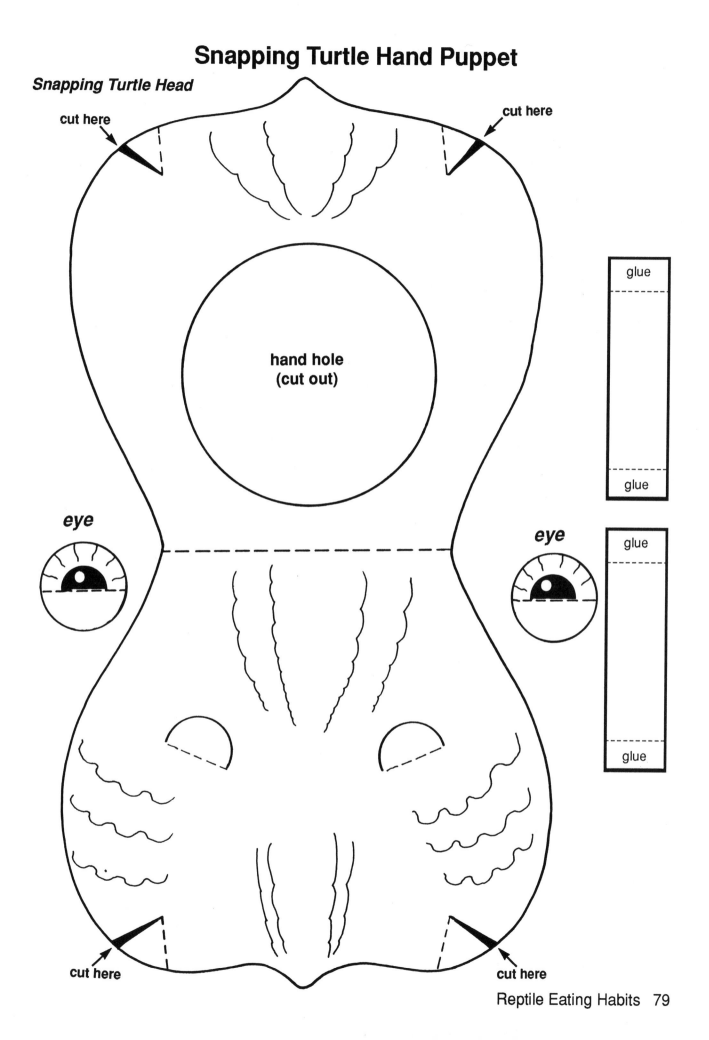

cut here

cut here

**hand hole
(cut out)**

glue

glue

eye

eye

glue

glue

cut here

cut here

Sea Turtle Mini-Book

4. The sun warms the sand on the eggs. The turtles grow inside the eggs.

This animal mini-book was made by:

_____

5. Baby turtles hatch from the eggs and dig their way out of the sand.

6. The baby turtles crawl down into the sea. They swim away.

2. She lays her eggs in the hole.

1. A female sea turtle comes out of the water. She digs a hole in the sand.

3. The turtle covers her eggs with sand.

STAPLE HERE

**How a
Sea Turtle
Is Hatched**

Alligator Grows Up Pop-Up Card

glue head here

glue tail here

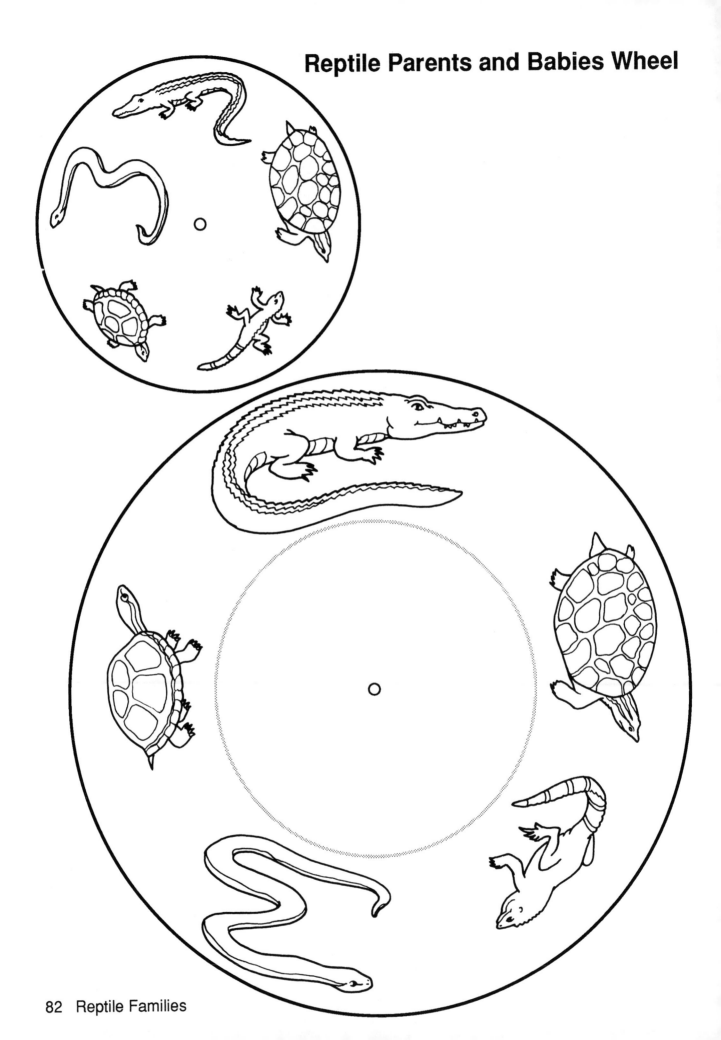

Chapter 4: BIRDS

Teacher: Use these facts with your class to stimulate discussion and to create big books, fact wheels, posters, and bulletin boards. Reproduce the facts chart below for children to use for reference.

What You Should Know About Birds
- Birds are the only animals with feathers.
- Birds breathe with lungs and have air sacs.
- Birds are warm-blooded.
- Birds have scales on their legs and feet.
- Most birds can fly.
- Birds have hard beaks instead of teeth.
- Birds have hollow or partly hollow bones.
- Examples: robin, duck, penguin, wren, woodpecker, eagle, hummingbird.

Birds in the Wild
- Birds' arms are called "wings."
- Birds keep their feathers clean and neat. Most birds have an oil gland that helps them keep their feathers nice. Some birds take a bath in water.
- Birds sing to find a mate or to warn others to keep away.
- Water birds have skin between their toes. They use their feet as paddles in water.

Bird Eating Habits
- Birds use their beaks to eat and drink.
- Birds have different kinds of beaks because they eat different foods.
- Many birds fly long distances (migrate) to find food and shelter during the year.

Bird Families
- Most birds build nests when they mate.
- Female birds lay eggs in nests.
- Baby birds hatch from eggs.
- Most birds take care of their babies.
- Parents use their beaks to feed their babies until they learn to feed themselves.
- Parents keep the babies warm and safe as the babies grow feathers.
- When baby birds learn to fly, they leave the nest and live alone.

Teacher Page

The numbers shown after the titles indicate pages where patterns and assembly directions (**bold**) are found.

What You Should Know About Birds

Big Book and Bulletin Board Birds (pp. 86–88, **134**): Use the pictures on these pages to start your study of birds. You may want to reduce or enlarge them to be more in proportion. The facts on the preceding page will help you guide classroom discussions.

Bird Feet Match and Sort Cards (pp. 89–91, **138**): A bird's feet tell us how they have adapted to live in their habitats. **Perchers** (robin and dove) have three toes in front and one toe in back for gripping tree branches. **Scratchers** (pheasant and chicken) have toes like rakes for scratching in dirt. **Graspers** (hawk and owl) have curved claws that help them hold on tight to their prey. **Climbers** (woodpecker and cuckoo) have two front toes and two back toes for climbing on tree trunks. **Swimmers** (duck and goose) have skin between their toes to help them paddle through water. **Runners** (ostrich and killdeer) have toes that all point forward so they can run. {To use the cards, reproduce them on oak tag. Cut them apart on the heavy black lines and the gray lines. Mix them up and have children put them back together.}

Bird in Flight Flip Book (p. 92, **136**): Birds flap their wings to fly. Tiny hummingbirds flap their wings very fast. Large birds like eagles do not have to flap their wings so much. They can glide through the sky because of their wide wingspans. {When the book is completed, children can flip through it to see how a bird flaps its wings to fly.}

Why Birds Fly Puzzle (p. 93, **135**): Birds use their gift of flight in many ways. They fly up into trees to build their nests. Birds fly long distances (migrate) to live in warm climates. They look for food on the ground or catch food in the air. They fly to escape from enemies. {Children can point out ways birds use flight in the picture. Cut the picture into a puzzle and reassemble.}

Birds in the Wild

Fold-a-Bird Mobile Color-by-Number (pp. 94–96, **135**): Many people love to identify birds by the colors and markings on their feathers. Some birds are all one color (crow), while others have many colors on different parts of their bodies. {Some children may need help drawing in the different areas to color. Hang your classroom aviary from strings so that all can enjoy them and learn to identify many species by their colors.}

Shore Birds Lift-and-Look (pp. 97–98, **138**): Shore birds live near lakes, rivers, and marshes. Many can swim underwater to feed. They eat water plants, grain, seeds, or fish. Some have webbed feet to help them paddle in the water. Others have long legs for wading. Shore birds usually nest on dry land.

Perching and Climbing Birds Lift-and-Look (pp. 99–100, **138**): Perching birds live in trees. They can clasp their feet around branches or grab into bark with their claws. Most perching birds are fine singers. Most migrate to warm weather to find food and to breed.

Bird Eating Habits

Bird Beaks Fact Wheel (p. 101, **136**): Just as bird feet tell us about bird habits, their beaks tell us more. A **toucan** has a very long, strong beak for plucking fruit from trees. The **flamingo** has a beak that strains tiny plants and animals from water. The **pelican** has a beak with a pouch that it uses to scoop up a mouthful of fish. The **hummingbird** has a narrow, hollow beak to drink nectar from the inside of flowers. The **warbler** picks insects from leaves and logs with its sharp beak. The **whip-poor-will** flies through the air to catch insects in its wide mouth. The **snipe** catches worms and other small animals in its mouth by digging in mud and water. {Assemble the wheel and let children turn it to match beaks with birds. Talk about why beaks are useful to birds.}

Bird Food Picture Cube (p. 102, **140**): After becoming familiar with the Bird Beaks Fact Wheel, children can roll the cube like a die, then find a bird on the wheel that eats the sort of food that is shown on the top of the cube.

Be-a-Bird Owl Mask (p. 103, **138**): Owls fly at night to find small animals to eat. They grab mice with their feet and fly away to have dinner. An owl has big eyes which help it see in the dark.

Bird Families

Bird Mini-Book (p. 104, **139**): This book tells a typical story of birds nesting and hatching babies. Parents keep babies warm in the nest. They feed them. They protect them from enemies. They teach them to fly. They teach them to find their own food. {After the books are assembled by the class, read the story and talk about ways that birds help their babies. }

Blue Jay Cup Puppet (p. 105, **135**): **Jays** are outgoing birds. They eat insects and seeds (omnivorous). Baby jays know to open their mouths to get food when their parents come to the nest.

Birds and Nests Lace-Ups (pp. 106–108, **137**): Birds build many different shapes and kinds of nests. The lace-ups show several kinds. Birds gather materials for their nests and build them in a certain way. They use the nests for hatching baby birds.

Bird Crafts

Here are two simple ways for children to recycle some common household items and care for their wildlife neighbors, the birds! Other projects can be found in some of the books listed in the bibliography. There are no patterns for these activities.

Egg Carton Bird Feeders (135): Birds appreciate finding food easily and you can help them. Assemble the bird feeders and hang them in the school yard or let children take them home. Once the birds start to use the feeder, be sure to replace the food regularly!

Nest Builder Board (139): In spring, birds start to build their nests. Providing them with building materials will help you attract birds to your area. Birds will fly by and take the strings and lint to build their nests.

Big Book and Bulletin Board Birds

red-tailed hawk

Big Book and Bulletin Board Birds

ostrich

Big Book and Bulletin Board Birds

varied thrush

Bird Feet Match and Sort Cards

woodpecker

cut ✂

climber

cuckoo

climber

ostrich

cut ✂

runner

killdeer

runner

Bird Feet Match and Sort Cards

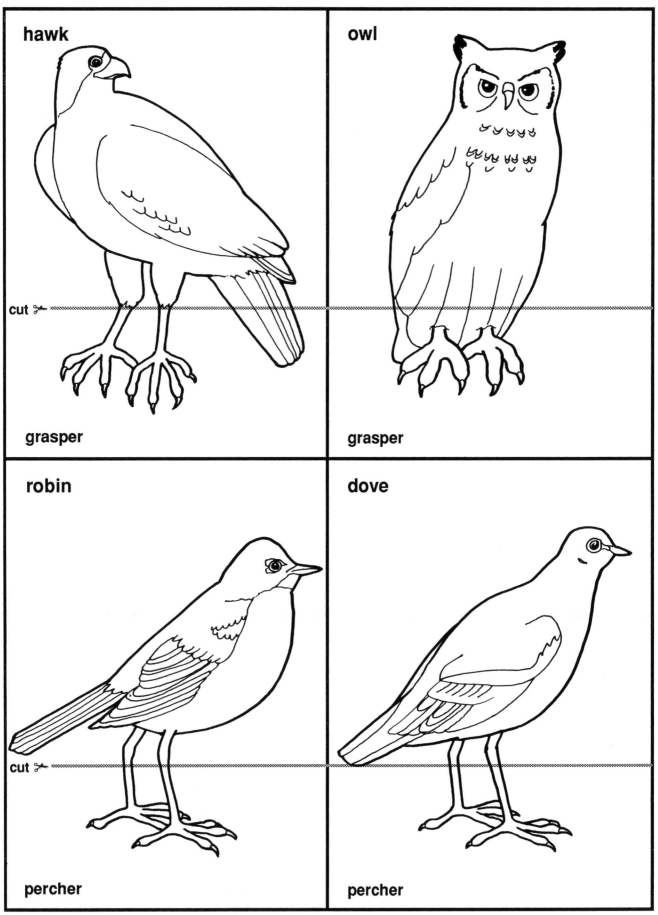

hawk

cut ✂

grasper

owl

grasper

robin

cut ✂

percher

dove

percher

Bird Feet Match and Sort Cards

pheasant

scratcher

chicken

scratcher

duck

swimmer

goose

swimmer

cut

cut

Bird in Flight Flip Book

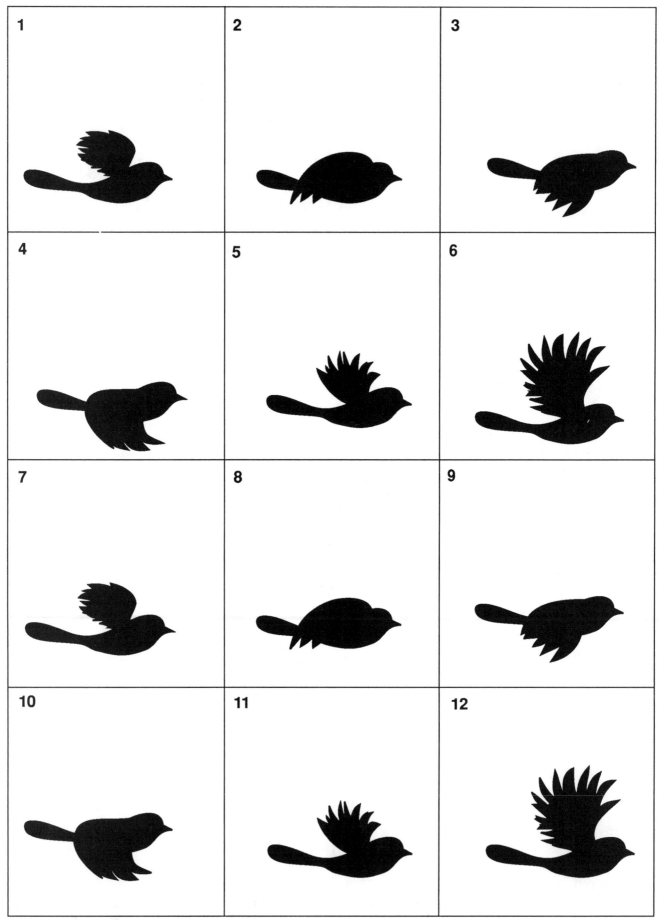

Why Birds Fly Puzzle

Color-by-Number Fold-A-Bird Mobile

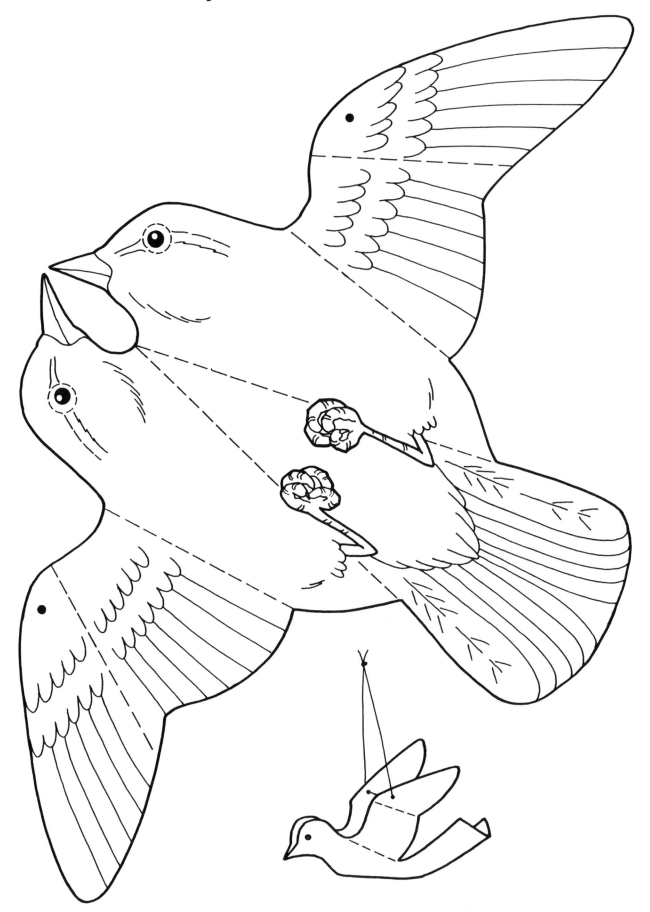

Color-by-Number Fold-A-Bird Mobile

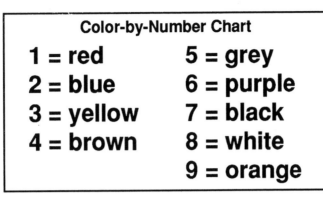

Color-by-Number Chart

1 = red	5 = grey
2 = blue	6 = purple
3 = yellow	7 = black
4 = brown	8 = white
	9 = orange

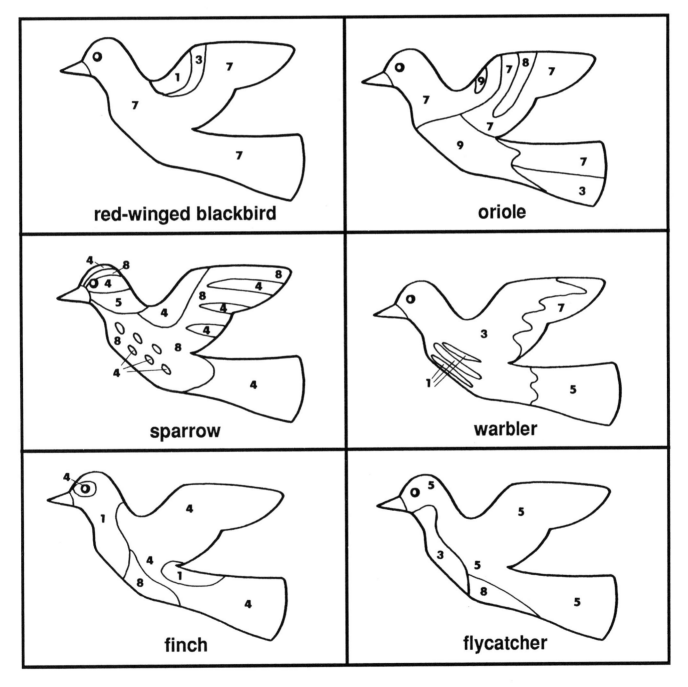

red-winged blackbird

oriole

sparrow

warbler

finch

flycatcher

Color-by-Number Fold-A-Bird Mobile

nuthatch

catbird

bluebird

robin

goldfinch

woodpecker

purple martin

wren

Shore Birds Lift-and-Look

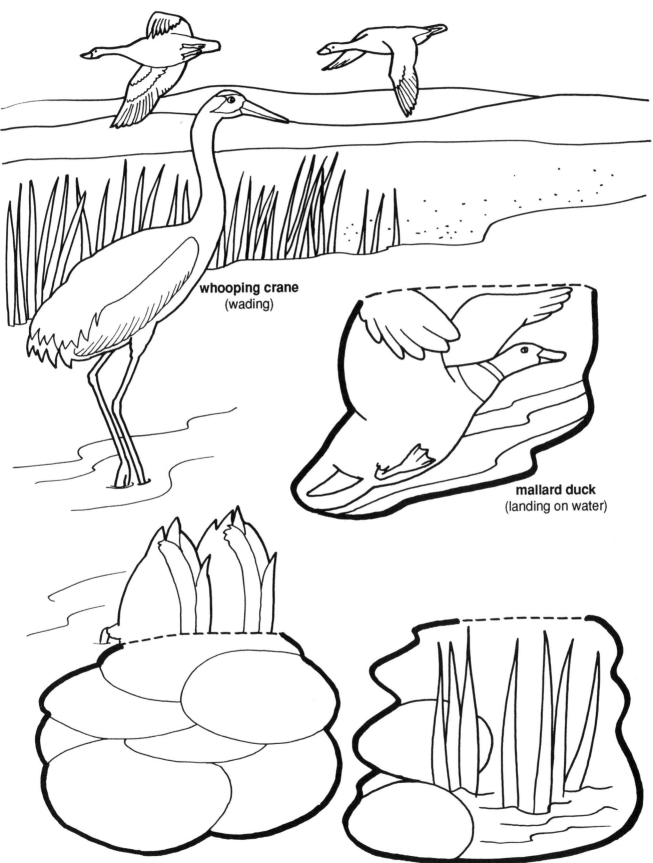

geese (flying)

whooping crane
(wading)

mallard duck
(landing on water)

Shore Birds Lift-and-Look

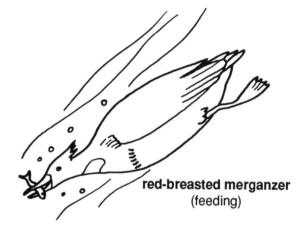

red-breasted merganzer
(feeding)

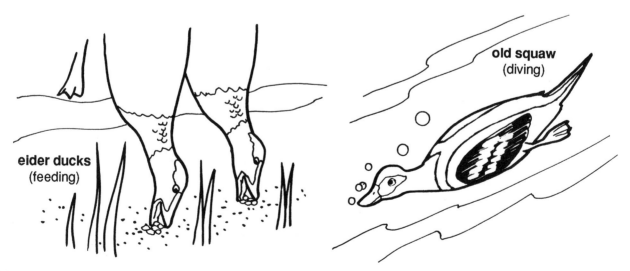

eider ducks
(feeding)

old squaw
(diving)

Perching Birds Lift-and-Look

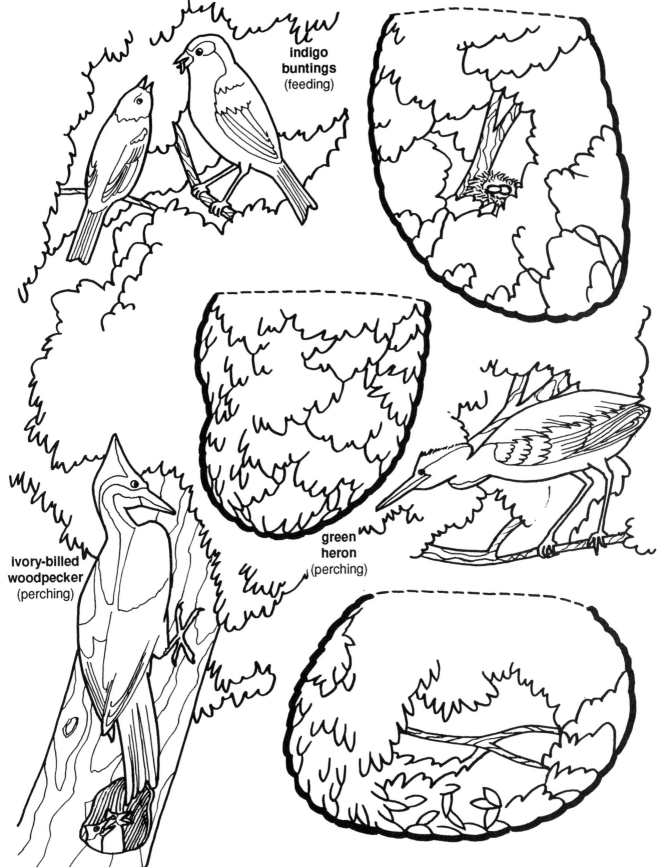

indigo
buntings
(feeding)

ivory-billed
woodpecker
(perching)

green
heron
(perching)

Perching Birds Lift-and-Look

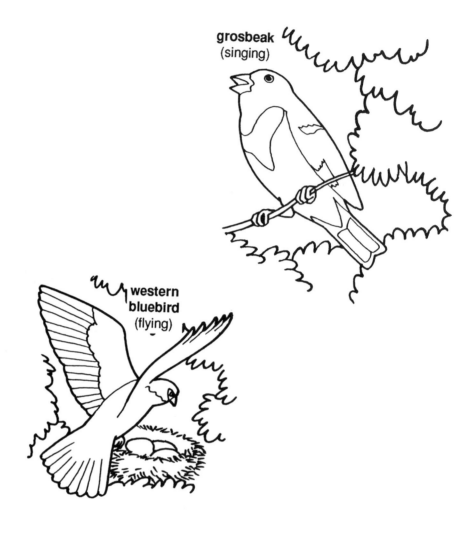

grosbeak
(singing)

western bluebird
(flying)

belted kingfisher
(feeding)

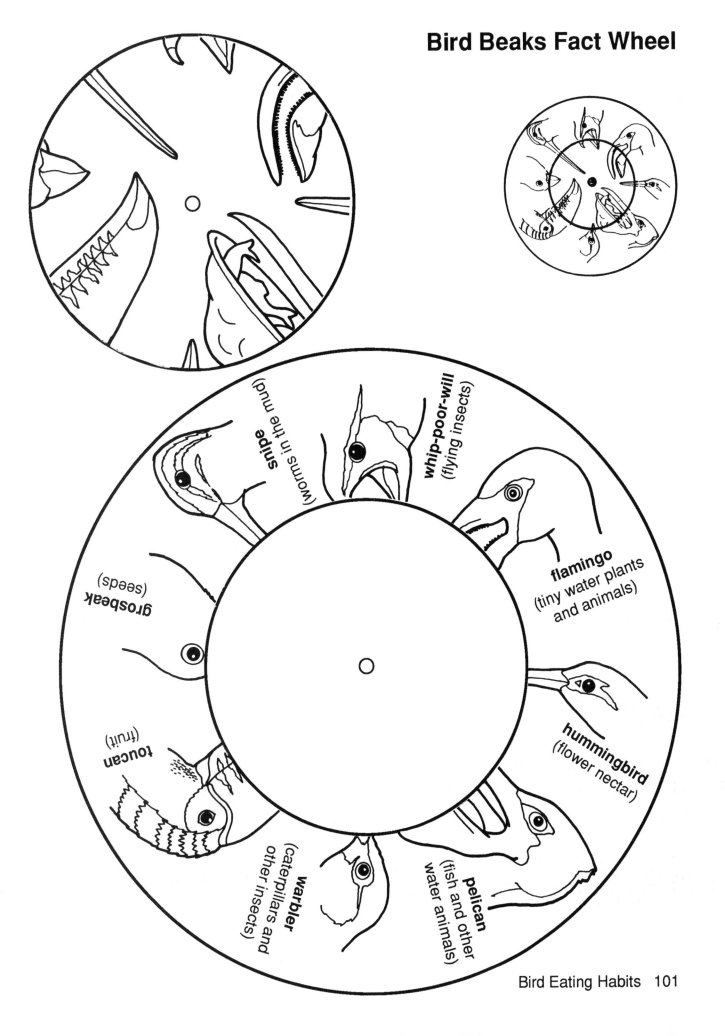

whip-poor-will
(flying insects)

snipe
(worms in the mud)

flamingo
(tiny water plants
and animals)

grosbeak
(seeds)

hummingbird
(flower nectar)

toucan
(fruit)

warbler
(caterpillars and
other insects)

pelican
(fish and other
water animals)

Bird Food Picture Cube

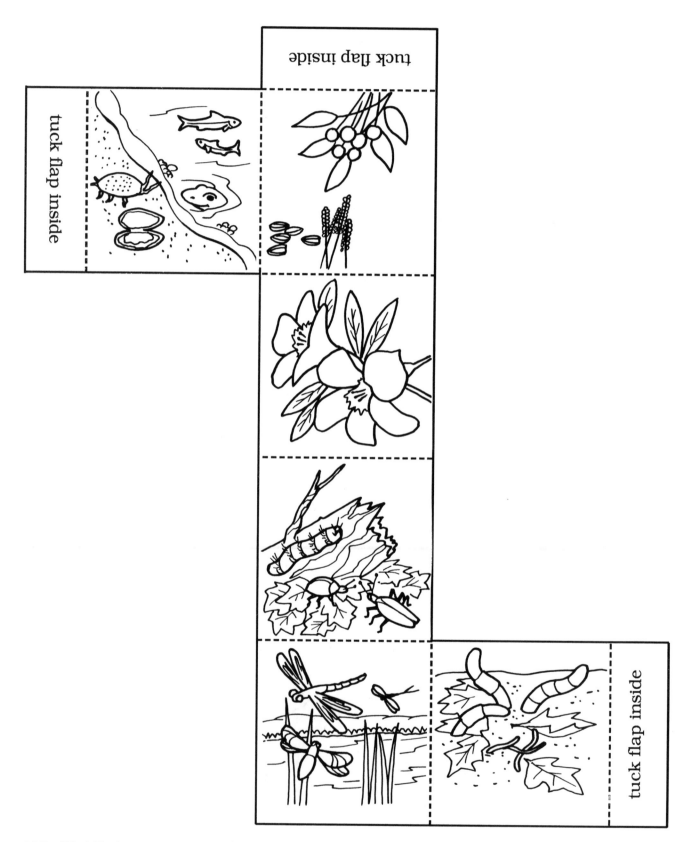

Owl Mask

Bird Mini-Book

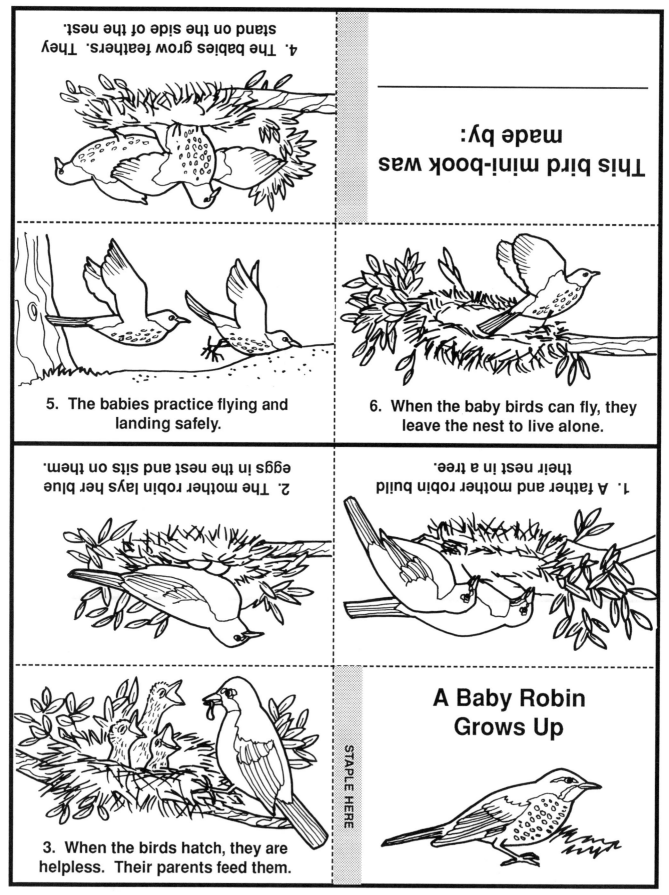

4. The babies grow feathers. They stand on the side of the nest.

This bird mini-book was made by:

5. The babies practice flying and landing safely.

6. When the baby birds can fly, they leave the nest to live alone.

2. The mother robin lays her blue eggs in the nest and sits on them.

1. A father and mother robin build their nest in a tree.

STAPLE HERE

3. When the birds hatch, they are helpless. Their parents feed them.

A Baby Robin Grows Up

Blue Jay Cup Puppet

glue here

Birds and Nests Lace-Ups

elf owl

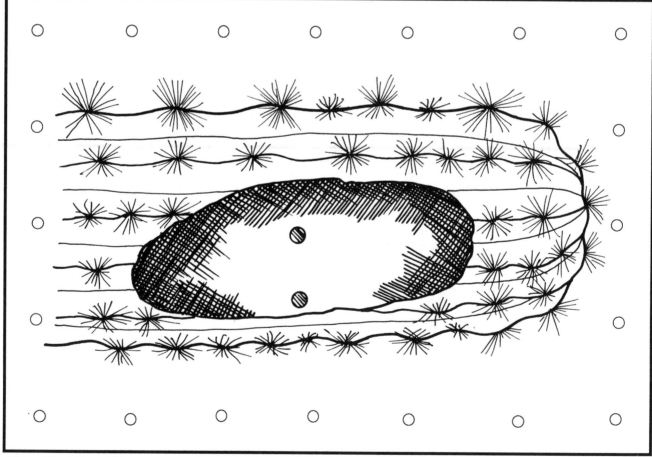

Birds and Nests Lace-Ups

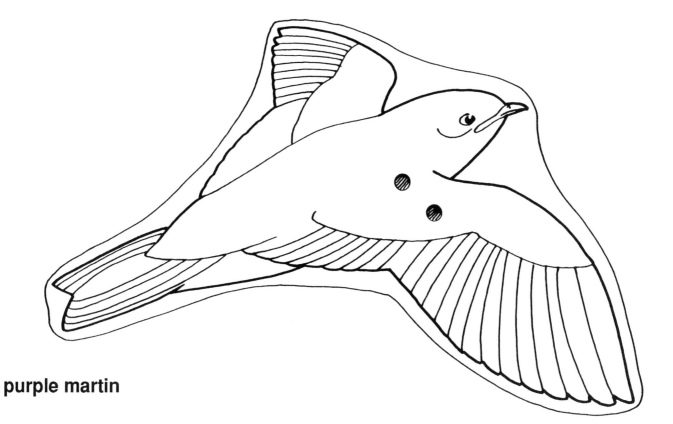

purple martin

Birds and Nests Lace-Ups

bald eagle

Chapter 5: ANIMALS AND THEIR HABITATS

Teacher: Use these fact cards on the following pages with your class to stimulate discussion about various animal habitats and to create big books, fact wheels, posters, and bulletin boards. Readers may use them as reference to create other projects. The numbers shown in parentheses indicate pages where patterns and assembly directions **(bold)** are found.

Wetland Environment Facts

- Wetlands, also called bogs, marshes, or swamps, are very soggy.
- Wetlands are an important home for many animals.
- Sometimes animals live in wetlands to raise their young (duck).
- Many animals come to the wetlands to hunt for food (deer, mink).
- Saltwater marshes provide food for ocean animals as tides go out (dolphin).
- Wetlands help control flooding. High-river waters can overflow into marshes.
- Native Americans were the first to use the important resources of wetlands.
- Wetlands help clean up pollution by spreading it out and filtering it.
- Dumping sewage, garbage, and filling land, endangers wetlands.
- Laws have been made to protect and preserve wetlands.

Wetland Activities

Freshwater Marsh Theatre (pp. 113–114, 141): Many animals hide among the rushes and grasses for protection or from habit. The **wood duck**, a colorful bird, lives in wooded swamps and nests in tree hollows. The **mink** lives all across the United States and Canada. It snatches up frogs, birds, and fish while swimming. The **red-tailed hawk's** tail is rusty orange. It eats small animals. The **white-tailed deer** is reddish brown except for its tail. It eats grasses, apples, acorns, and fungi. Good swimmers and leapers (30 feet), they are active day and night.

Mangrove Swamp Theatre (pp. 115–116, 141): The waters move less than in a regular saltwater marsh. Less oxygen is available for the plants that grow there. Tiny organisms use oxygen to decompose. Instead of marsh grasses, animals depend upon the mangrove trees growing there. Above the water, animals make their nests and rest in them. Below, the water animals feed and hide among the weedy roots that spread out into the water. Plants anchor in the mud and gather as much oxygen as possible. The **bronze frog**, named for its color, is secretive and hard to find in southern swamps. The **alligator** is the largest reptile. It can hide in water because its eyes and nose are on top of the head, allowing it to see and breathe while waiting to catch small animals. It uses its long tail to swim and as a whip for protection. The **red-bellied turtle** is native to southern swamps. It likes to bask in the sun on a log or a rock. The **grizzly bear** is large and ferocious. It uses its sharp claws and teeth for protection and to tear food. It eats insects, fish, plants, and small mammals. Its coat varies from yellowish-brown to almost black. Bears are the largest land-living carnivores.

Preserve the Wetlands Pencil Toppers (p. 117, 140): Wetlands are vitally necessary for our overall environmental protection against pollution and erosion. Many plants strain or absorb harmful pollutants out of water, making water cleaner. Wetlands allow water to spread over large areas to prevent flooding and erosion of farmlands and other developed areas.

Ocean Environment Facts

- Oceans cover more of the earth than land.
- Dissolved rocks and minerals make ocean water salty.
- Other minerals (gold, silver, calcium, magnesium) are in the ocean, too.
- Saltwater is recycled daily as it evaporates, rises, and falls as rain.
- Ocean water is in motion from hot and cold currents, waves, and tides.
- The bottom of the ocean isn't flat. It has mountains, hills, valleys, and plains.
- Kelp forests in oceans are homes and food to many ocean animals.
- Ocean water is cold. More than half is colder than 36 degrees.
- Plastics can make oceans unsafe for animals living there. Some animals eat the plastic. Others get tangled or strangled by it.
- Laws have been made to stop people from throwing garbage into our oceans.

Ocean Activities

Arctic Seashore Theatre (pp. 118–119, **141**): The rocky shoreline is home to many hardy birds and mammals. They have each adapted to cold temperatures. **Northern gannets** nest in large colonies along seashores. They feed by diving fifty or more feet in the ocean. **Puffins** spend the winter at sea. They are water birds with webbed feet like ducks. The **ringed seal** is the smallest seal, about five feet long. It is very awkward on land but is an excellent swimmer in the Arctic Ocean. The **polar bear** has a yellowish-white coat of fur. An excellent swimmer, it stalks birds, seals and other sea animals. The **fulmar** lives far out at sea in the northern Atlantic and Pacific Oceans. It comes to shore to nest on high sea cliffs. The female lays only one egg.

Open Sea Theatre (pp. 120–121, **141**): Three-quarters of the earth is covered with oceans, homes to some of the largest mammals. The **sperm whale** grows up to sixty feet long and can dive a mile down into the ocean. It can hold its breath for up to seventy-five minutes. It feeds on squid and cuttlefish, eating up to a ton of food a day. The **blue shark** feeds on fishes at the bottom of the ocean. It is eight feet long and has a reputation as a "man-eater." The **bottle-nosed dolphin** is often seen near shore. It is easily trained and often seen at aquatic shows. It "talks" in chirps, squeaks, and whistles. The **black guillemot** comes to shore only to nest in northern Canada. It can swim underwater using its wings. The **pilot whale**, about twenty feet long, gets its name because it often follows a lead whale. It works with other pilot whales to help fight off enemies. The **common porpoise** is one the most intelligent animals in the world. It makes its way in the ocean using sonar called *echolocation*. It communicates with other porpoises by making clicking and whistling sounds. It is a very fast swimmer.

Save Our Oceans Poster (p. 122): Reproduce a poster page for each student or group. Color and cut out the pieces and use with colored papers, magazine pictures, or other materials to create eye-catching posters. Display with your theatres or in other areas of your classroom. Note: The patterns can also be used for mobiles or dioramas.

Rain Forest Environment Facts

- Rain forests have hot, humid, rainy weather all year round. They are the wettest lands in the world.
- Rain forests can get 200" of rain yearly and stay at 70°–85° Farenheit.
- Plants grow tall, making a canopy of branches high in the forest.
- Few plants grow on the ground since sunshine cannot get through.
- More than half of all the earth's species live in the rain forest. New species are being discovered each year.
- Rain forests are rich with life, but they are very fragile environments.
- Cutting, burning, or over-harvesting the rain forest trees destroys this habitat.
- Many plants and animals cannot live anywhere but in the rain forest.
- People living in rain forests must be protected too. Their knowledge of the rain forest could help us develop new medicines from plants or to discover new foods from animals and plants that could feed hungry people everywhere.

Rain Forest Activities

Rain Forest Theatre (pp. 123–126, **141**): The top of the rain forest (**emergent layer**) rises over 250 feet where many types of trees compete for sunlight. At 65–100 feet is a thick carpet of trees called the **canopy**. Many species of animals live in this area; they climb thick vines, swing from tree to tree, and never go down to the forest floor! The **forest floor** gets little sunlight, so it has fewer plants. The **royal antelope**, the smallest antelope in the world, lives in West Africa. Adults stand about fifteen inches high. They feed on leaves and fruit. They are very shy and rarely seen. The **cuscus**, a marsupial, lives in New Guinea. It uses its grasping tail to climb from limb to limb and to find food. The **pangolin** of Asia and Africa uses its sharp claws to dig into ant and termite nests. Its scaly body acts as an armor to protect it from enemies. The **emerald tree boa** of South America is an excellent climber. It can wrap itself around tree branches. The **morpho butterfly** of Central and South America flits through jungle trees. Its underside is a dull brown, but the wing tops are a beautiful, bright blue. The **tapir's** black and white coat helps it hide on the forest floor. It uses its nose to find food. It lives in southeast Asia. The **marine toad**, weighing up to two pounds, lives along the banks of the Amazon River. It eats insects, plants, and dead animals. The **orangutan** lives in Borneo and Sumatra. It spends its time in the canopy searching for fruit, shoots, and leaves. Its strong arms are for swinging from tree to tree. At night it sleeps in a nest of branches and leaves. The **capybara** from Brazil is the largest rodent. It eats plants found in and near water. The **three-toed sloth** in Central and South America moves slowly, using its sharp claws to grip tree branches. It hangs upside down to sleep and to eat leaves and fruits. {Because the rain forest is more varied than other habitats, assemble the theatre by putting both pages together. The puppets will be used around the outside of the theatre. Note: Animals that live in the upper areas of the trees are stick puppets. Animals who live on the forest floor are stand-ups.}

Preserve the Rain Forest Buttons (p. 127): Reproduce on oaktag, color and cut out. Use safety pins to attach to clothing. Wear or share with other classrooms. These also make nice classroom incentives or gifts for family members. This is one way that children can help everyone learn to protect rain forests.

Desert Environment Facts

- Deserts are the driest habitats (less than 10" of rainfall per year).
- Deserts are hot all day and cold at night.
- Plants and animals must protect themselves from heat and cold.
- Plants grow tiny leaves, thick spines, and have deep roots.
- Many reptiles can live in the desert because of their thick skin and scales.
- Birds and mammals rest during the hot days and hunt at night when it's cooler.
- Deserts are very windy.
- Over-grazing sheep or cattle causes erosion and loss of desert plants.
- Cacti are home and food for some desert animals (elf owl, pack rat, iguana).
- Special parks protect desert plants and animal habitats.

Desert Activities:

Desert Theatre and Puppets (pp. 128–129, **141**): The desert scene shows rocks rounded and curved from desert erosion by water and wind. The **kit fox** feeds on desert rodents, insects, and birds. It will hunt at night and carry its prey to its den. Its large ears radiate heat to help it keep cool. The **owl** makes its nest inside a cactus and feeds at night. The **coyote** is also active at night. It hunts prey similar to the fox, but will also eat fruit. It is a swift, intelligent hunter with an excellent sense of smell and strong jaws. The **bobcat** (also called wildcat) is a small, fearless hunter. The **lizard's** scaly skin protects it from the sun, so it can tolerate higher temperatures. The **snake** burrows into the sand. The **coati**, related to the raccoon, travels in groups called bands and feeds on insects and some desert plants. The **scorpion**, related to spiders, is found only in warm climates and hunts insects and small mammals at night, paralyzing them with its stinging tail.

Friends of the Desert Stand-Ups (p. 130, **141**): Unusual landforms (columns, arch, and dunes) are created by desert winds, erosion, and rushing waters. {Reproduce enough stand-ups for each student. Ask students to color and cut them out. Display with your theatres or in other areas.}

Endangered Animal Facts

- People cause animals harm in four different ways:
  1. The habitat is changed, thus animals have nowhere to live.
  2. The habitat is polluted, thus animals have sick young or die.
  3. Animals are killed for food, skin, or sport until most are gone.
  4. Animals are moved to environments foreign to them. Having no natural defenses to fend them from hazards of their new habitats, the animals die.

Endangered Animal Activities:

Endangered Animal Dominoes (pp. 131–133, **136**): The animals included in the domino game are only a few of the familiar animals on the worldwide endangered list. In 1992, there were over 5,000 total species, including 698 mammals, 63 amphibians, 191 reptiles, 1,047 birds, 762 fishes, and 2,250 invertebrates. As world pollution increases and habitats, rich in wildlife, such as rain forests and wetlands decrease, more species will be at risk. Your students may be surprised to see many familiar zoo animals on the cards.

Freshwater Wetland Theatre

red-winged blackbird

great blue heron

beaver

frog

ducks

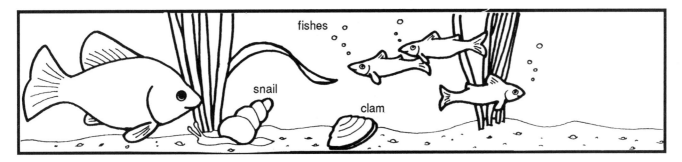

fishes

snail

clam

glue

fish

fiddler crab

mussels

Freshwater Wetland Puppets

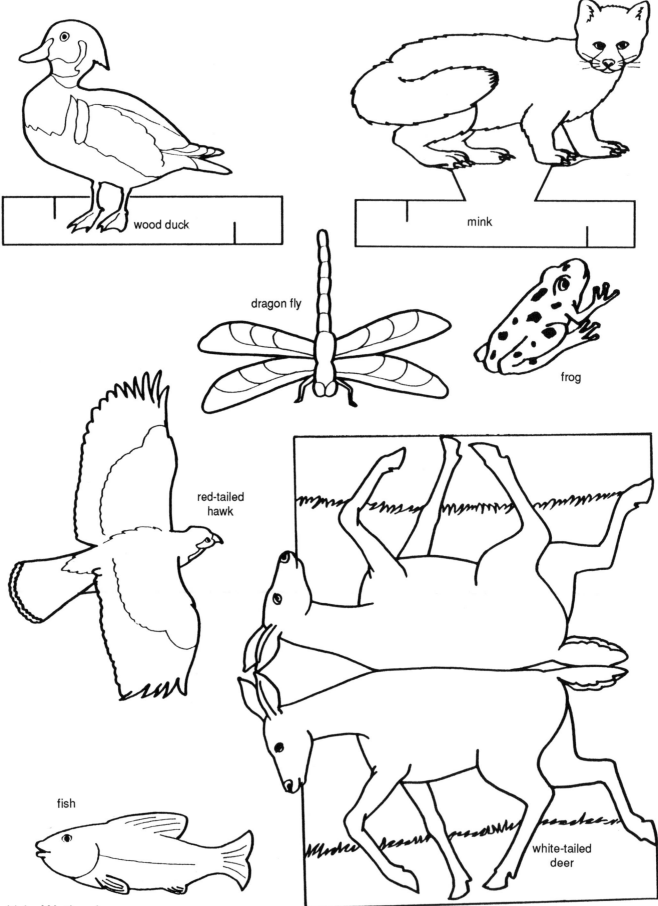

wood duck

mink

dragon fly

frog

red-tailed
hawk

fish

white-tailed
deer

Mangrove Swamp Theatre

Mangrove Swamp Puppets

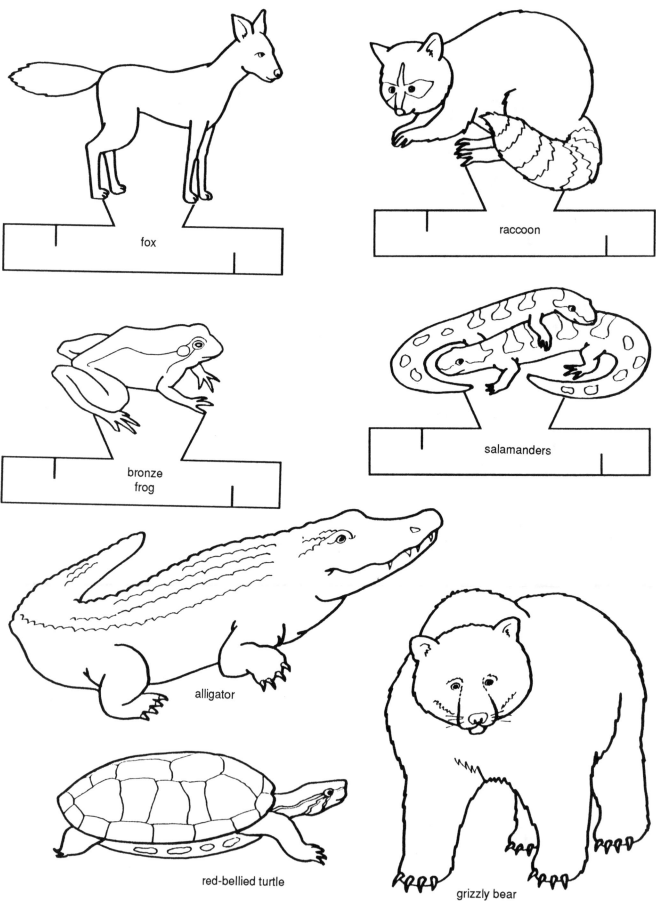

fox

raccoon

bronze
frog

salamanders

alligator

red-bellied turtle

grizzly bear

Preserve Our Wetlands Pencil Toppers

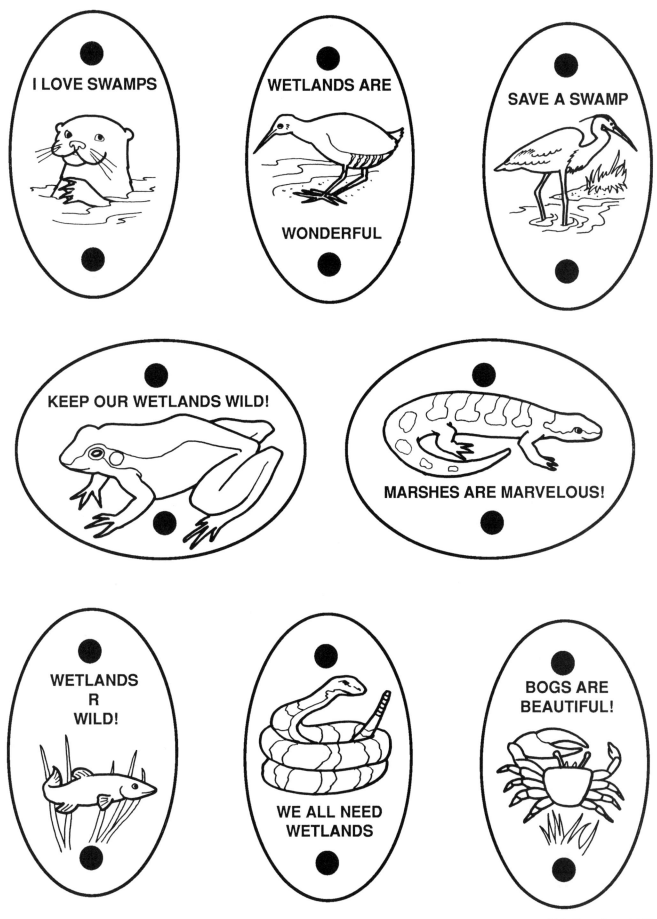

I LOVE SWAMPS

WETLANDS ARE

WONDERFUL

SAVE A SWAMP

KEEP OUR WETLANDS WILD!

MARSHES ARE MARVELOUS!

WETLANDS
R
WILD!

WE ALL NEED
WETLANDS

BOGS ARE
BEAUTIFUL!

Arctic Seashore Theatre

black cormorants

greater
yellow legs

killer whale

herring

bearded seal

glue

puffins

Arctic Seashore Puppets

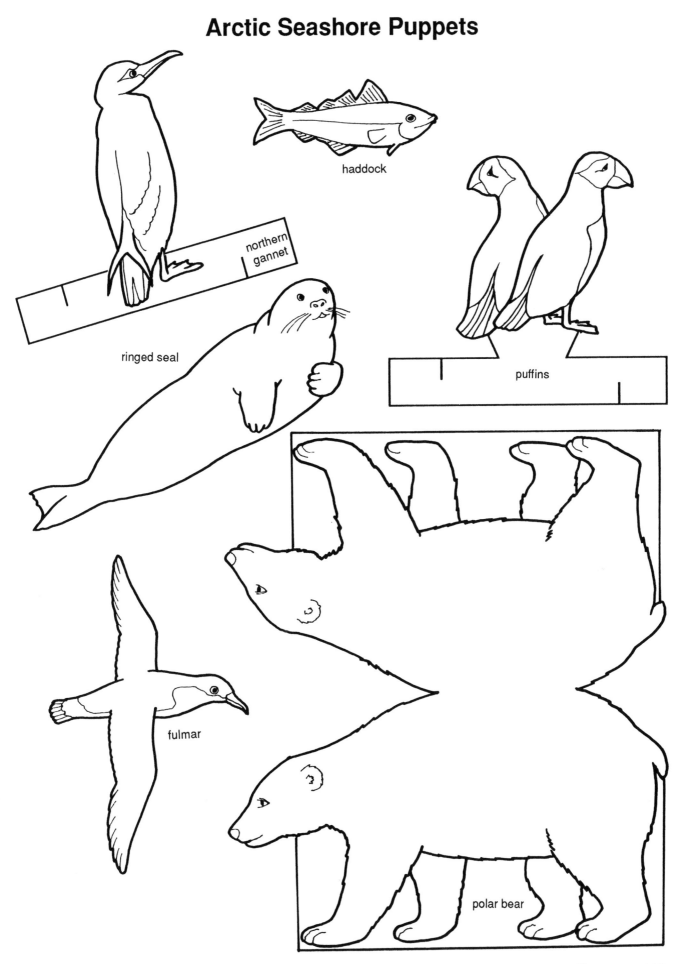

haddock

northern gannet

ringed seal

puffins

fulmar

polar bear

Open Sea Theatre

glaucous gull

manta ray

blue marlin

oceanic bonito

giant squid

dolphin fish

bluefin tuna

glue

Open Sea Puppets

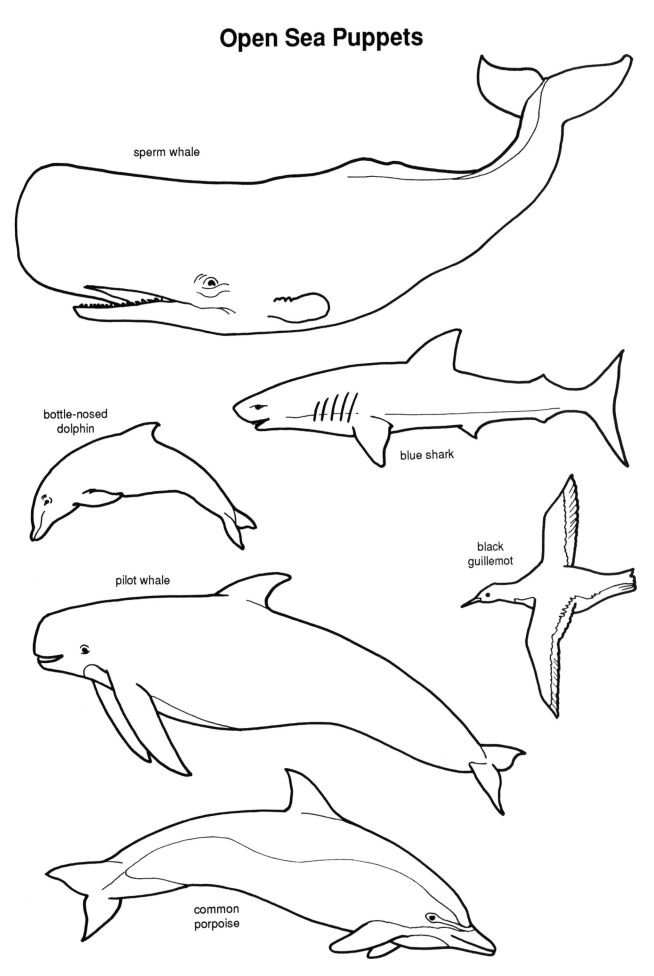

sperm whale

blue shark

bottle-nosed
dolphin

black
guillemot

pilot whale

common
porpoise

Save Our Oceans Poster Pieces

Text within images: KEEP OUR OCEANS CLEAN; SAVE OUR EARTH; EARTH IS A HOUSE THAT BELONGS TO US ALL; SAVE OUR OCEANS; SAVE OUR WHALES

Rain Forest Theatre

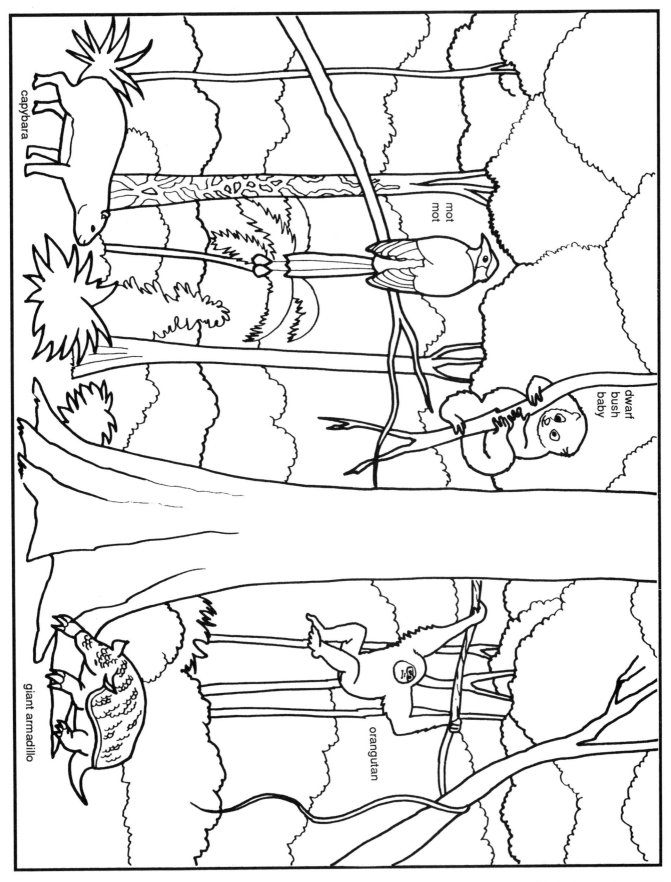

Rain Forest Theatre

glue

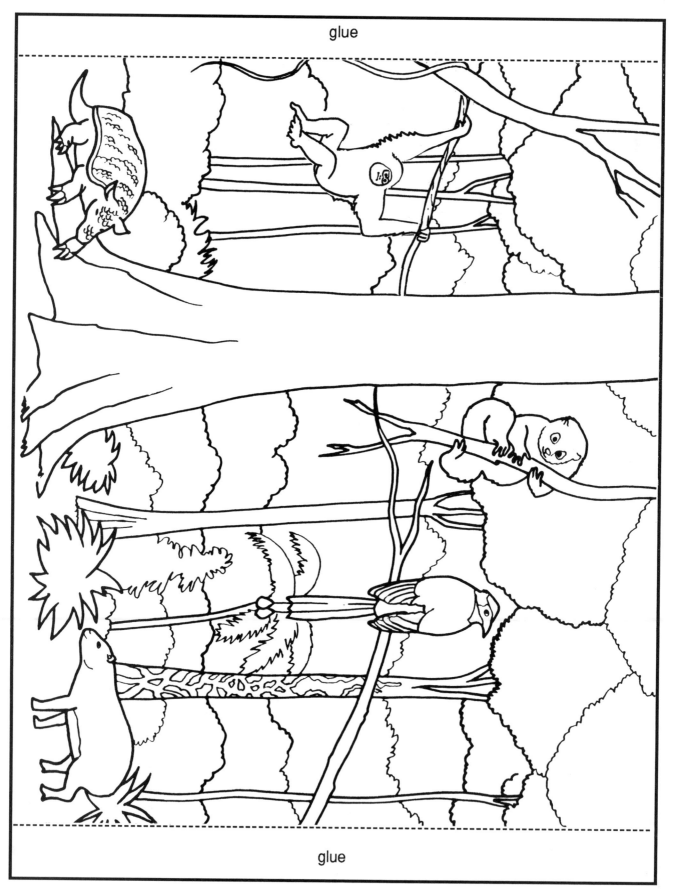

glue

Rain Forest Puppets

royal antelope

morpho butterfly

cuscus

emerald tree boa

pangolin

salamander

tapir

Rain Forest Puppets

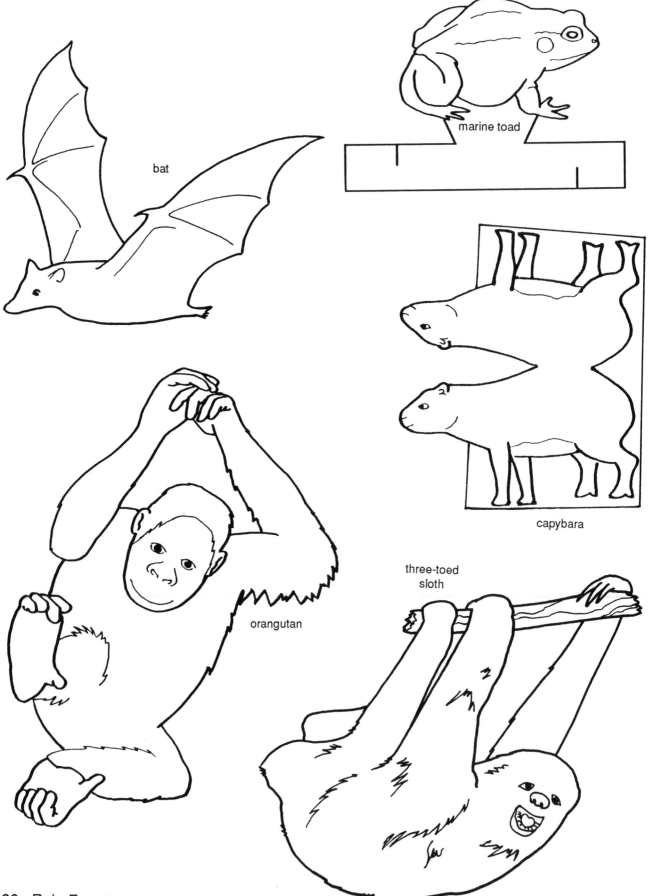

marine toad

bat

capybara

orangutan

three-toed
sloth

Protect the Rain Forest Buttons

LEARN–DON'T BURN!

PROTECT THE RAIN FOREST

SAVE THE WORLD FOR WILD THINGS!

SAVE OUR FOREST TREASURES!

EARTH DAY IS EVERY DAY

RAIN FORESTS KEEP OUR WORLD HEALTHY

Desert Theatre

glue

Desert Theatre Puppets

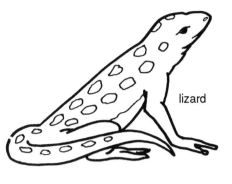
lizard

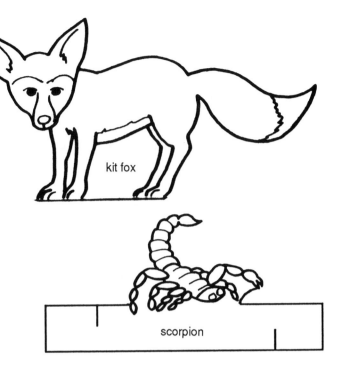
kit fox

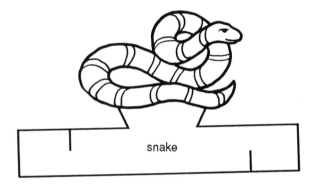
owl

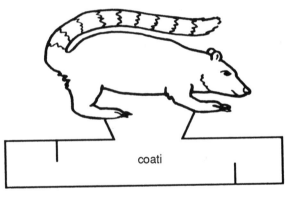
scorpion

snake

coati

bobcat

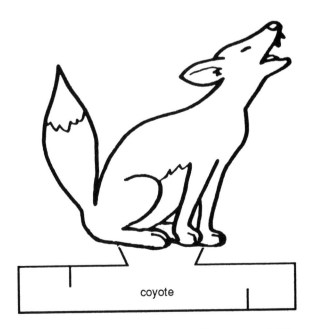
coyote

Friends of the Desert Stand-Ups

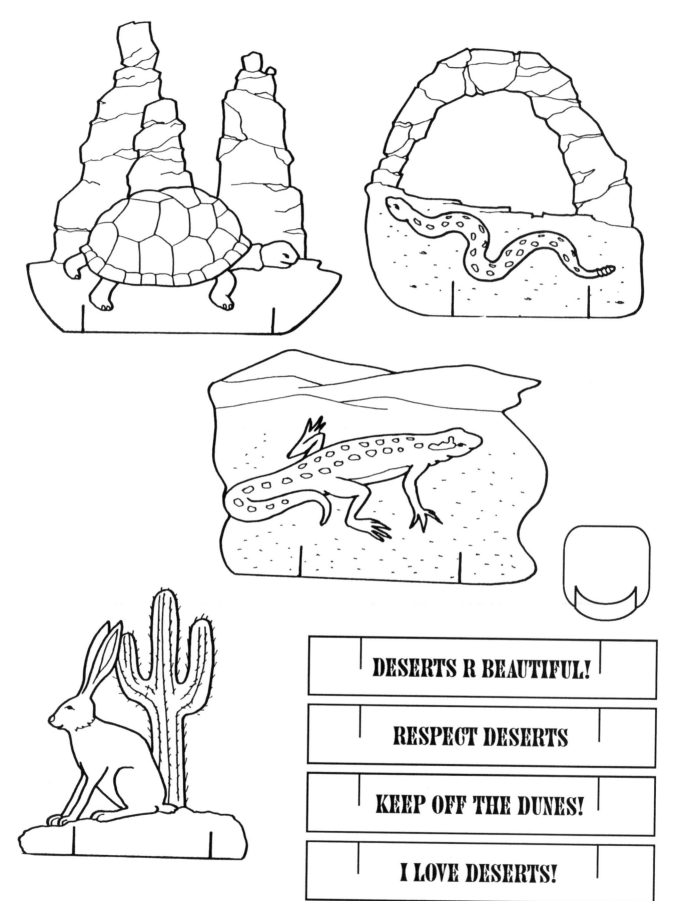

DESERTS R BEAUTIFUL!

RESPECT DESERTS

KEEP OFF THE DUNES!

I LOVE DESERTS!

Endangered Animals Dominoes

starter card

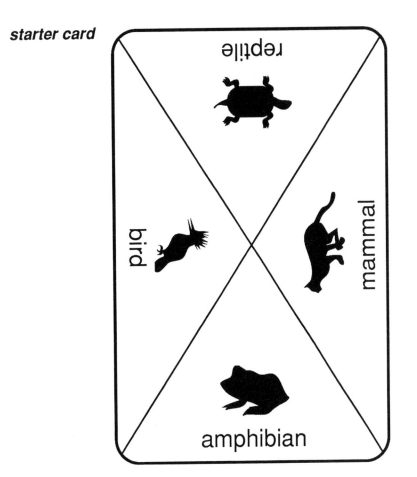

reptile

bird

mammal

amphibian

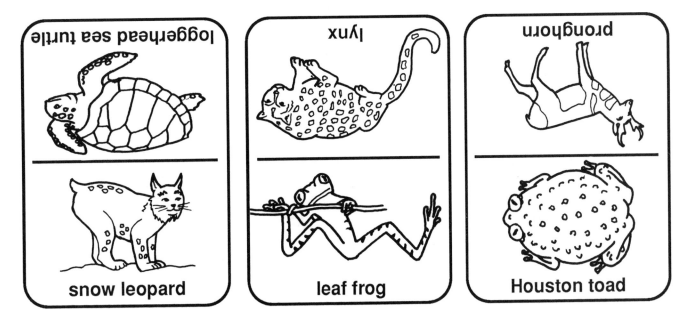

loggerhead sea turtle

lynx

pronghorn

snow leopard

leaf frog

Houston toad

Endangered Animals Dominoes

polar bear

iguana

gavial

Florida cougar

cheetah

puffin

Indian elephant

green sea turtle

mountain gorilla

paradise parrot

ibex

salt marsh snake

dingo

kiwi

prairie dog

Indian rhinoceros

black caiman

humpback whale

Endangered Animals Dominoes

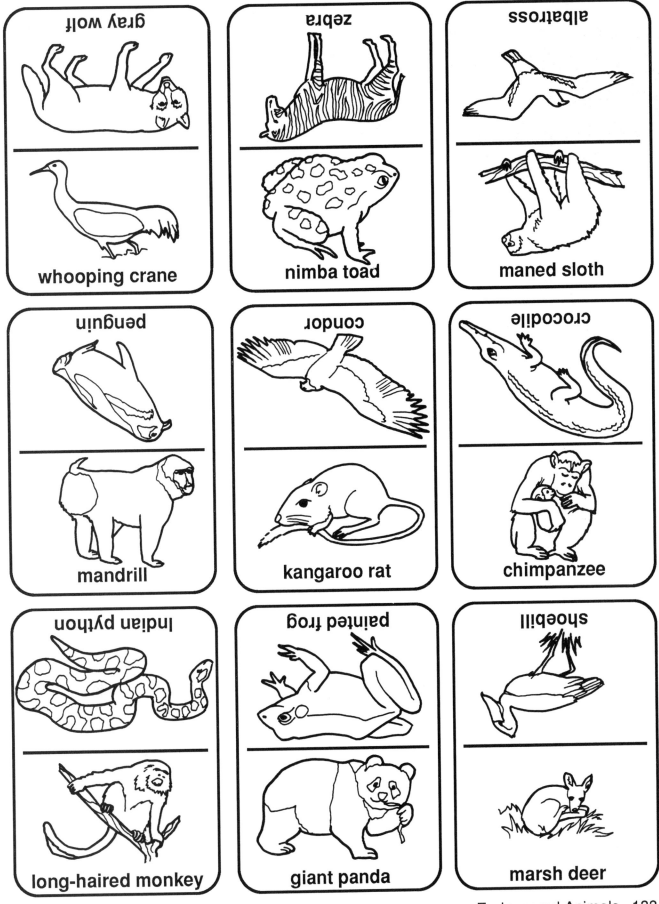

gray wolf

whooping crane

zebra

nimba toad

albatross

maned sloth

penguin

mandrill

condor

kangaroo rat

crocodile

chimpanzee

Indian python

long-haired monkey

painted frog

giant panda

shoebill

marsh deer

Directory of Animal Manipulatives

Teacher: Refer to the following directions to prepare for various projects throughout the book. A list of materials, how-to-make directions, and uses for each manipulative are included. You'll want to have all materials ready before presenting them to the class. The **Teacher Pages** at the beginning of each chapter have more information about each activity.

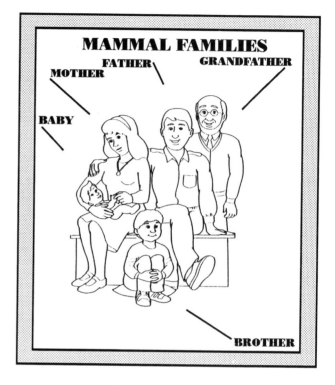

• Animals for Big Books or Bulletin Boards

Materials: white paper, animal patterns, scissors, crayons or markers

To Assemble:

1. Reproduce the patterns on white paper.
2. Color the animals and cut them out.

To Use: Put the animals on big book pages or on bulletin boards to introduce a particular group of animals. Add facts and more animal illustrations as you work through the chapters.

• Button Trails

Materials: lightweight cardboard or two sheets of oak tag, patterns, glue, scissors or art knife (for cutting trails), hole punch, large button, twist-tie, crayons or markers

To Assemble:

1. Reproduce the patterns on oak tag.
2. Color the trail scene and animal pattern, if desired.
3. Glue the trail and animal patterns to cardboard to make it sturdier.
4. Cut the trail with scissors or an art knife. Adult supervision is recommended.
5. Cut the animal pattern and punch holes as indicated.
6. Fold the twist-tie in half. Insert it in the animal holes and through the button holes. Twist ends to secure. (See illustration.)
7. Insert animal into trail with the button on the back of the trail sheet.

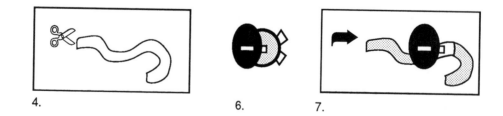

4. 6. 7.

• Color-by-Number Puzzles or Mobiles

Materials: oak tag, puzzle or mobile patterns, crayons, scissors, thread or fishing line

To Assemble:
1. Reproduce the puzzle or mobile on oak tag.
2. Color the animals as indicated by the Color Chart.
3. For puzzle: Cut out and reassemble.
4. For mobile: Cut out and fold as shown on the pattern pages.

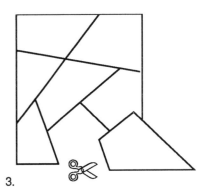

3.

• Cup Puppets

Materials: oak tag, cup puppet patterns, scissors, glue, small paper cup, ice-cream stick or tongue depressor, crayons or markers

To Assemble:
1. Reproduce all patterns on oak tag.
2. Color the pictures and cut them out.
3. Glue the cup pattern to to the paper cup.
4. Using the ice-cream stick, punch a hole through the bottom of the cup. (This step is not required for the Desert Cup Puppet.)
5. Glue the animal pattern to the ice-cream stick.

To Use: Move the animal inside the cup by moving the stick up and down. See the Teacher Pages at the beginning of each chapter for other ways to use the puppets.

• Egg Carton Bird Feeders

Materials: 1 plastic egg carton, hole punch, 12 teaspoons of peanut butter or ground suet, bag of bird seed (2 tablespoons for each of the cups to start), two 18" lengths of sturdy cord

To Assemble:
1. Cut the top from the egg carton and punch holes on the outside corners as shown.
2. String the cord through the holes and tie so that the cords are the same length.
3. Place a teaspoon of the peanut butter or suet in the bottom of each egg cup.
4. Press 1-2 tablespoons of the seeds into each cup.
5. Place the feeder on a level branch of a tree near a classroom window or remove the string and place feeder on a dry, protected window ledge.

For 12 Mini feeders: Cut apart the 12 egg cup sections. Use two 9"cords for each. Punch at the four corners, tie as shown. Fill and hang.

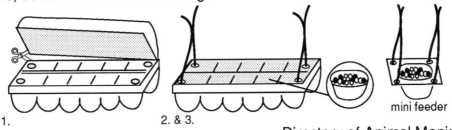

• Endangered Animals Dominoes

Materials: 1 set of cards reproduced on oak tag

Get Ready: Cut out all the cards. Put the **starter card** face up on the table. Mix up the other cards and place them face down in a pile where players can reach them.

To Play (for one or more players): Player draws one card from the pile and matches one end of the card to the starter card, next to the animal group it represents. Players continue to take turns drawing and matching animal groups (mammal to mammal, bird to bird, etc.). If the playing surface is limited, players may turn the cards in a different direction (see diagram). The game is over when all the animal dominoes have been placed.

Additional Play: Create more games using other categories of animals (flying, water, land, desert, wetlands, etc.). You can copy animals from other areas in this book, just cover the animals and type. Then, copy as many blank domino cards pages as you need.

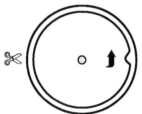

4. not all wheels have a notch

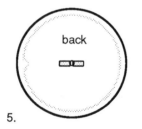

5.

• Fact/Expression Wheels

Materials: oak tag, wheel patterns, scissors, metal brad, crayons (optional)

To Assemble:
1. Reproduce the wheel patterns on oak tag.
2. Color the wheels with markers or crayons.
3. Cut out the wheels.
4. Place the smaller wheel on top of the larger wheel.
5. Insert brad in center. Open brad on back to secure.

To Use: Turn the wheel to match animals or to find facts as indicated in the Teacher Pages in each chapter.

• Flip Books

Materials: oak tag, flip book page pattern, scissors, stapler

To Assemble:
1. Reproduce the flip book page on oak tag.
2. Cut the flip book apart on the solid lines.
3. Stack the pages in order with 1 on top and 12 on the bottom.
4. Staple the flip book together at the top center, beside the number 1.

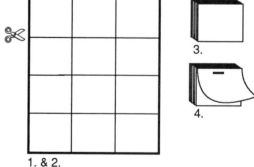

1. & 2.

3.

4.

To Use: Hold the flip book at the top with one hand. Flip through the bottom of the pages with the thumb of the other hand. See the animal move!

• Hand Puppets

Materials: oak tag, puppet patterns, scissors, glue or tape, crayons or markers

To Assemble:

1. Reproduce pattern pieces on oak tag.
2. Cut out all pieces as instructed and color (if desired).
3. Fold along dash lines.
4. Cut slits on head; overlap and glue to add a curve to the mouth (see diagram below).
5. Glue on eyes, ears, or other pieces (as indicated) to the head.
6. Glue finger tabs inside the mouth* so that when the child puts a hand through the hole, a finger can be slipped into each tab to open and close the jaws.
   *Glue tab ends to make a small curve in the middle for finger.
7. Glue body tab behind the head, inside the hand hole.

To Use: Put hand through the hand hole. Slip fingers into tabs inside mouth. Practice opening and shutting the jaws to make the animal "eat." Put the animal food into the puppet mouth.

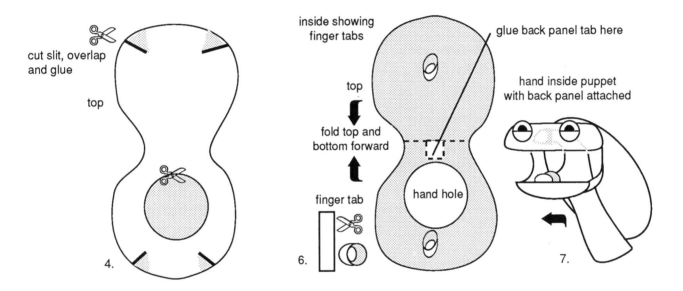

• Lace-Ups

Materials: oak tag, lace-up patterns, scissors, hole punch or pencil, 36" of curling ribbon or yarn, crayons or markers

To Assemble:

1. Reproduce patterns on oak tag.
2. Color, if desired.
3. Cut out and punch holes as indicated on lace-up.
4. Sew on the animal piece with ribbon or yarn. Continue sewing all around the card as shown in diagrams.

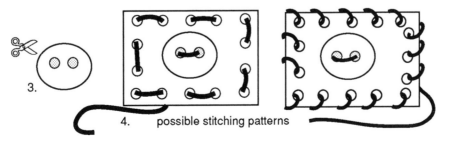

possible stitching patterns

• Lift-and-Look Pages

Materials: 8 1/2" x 11" bond paper, lift-and-look patterns, scissors, glue, crayons

To Assemble:
1. Reproduce pages on 8 1/2" x 11" bond paper.
2. Color the lift-and-look patterns.
3. Cut out the windows (solid line) on the top sheet. Fold on dashed lines.
4. Put glue on the **back** of the top sheet around the **outside margins**.
5. Place top sheet (with windows) on top of other sheet. Wait for glue to dry.

To Use: Lift the top pictures to see what is underneath.

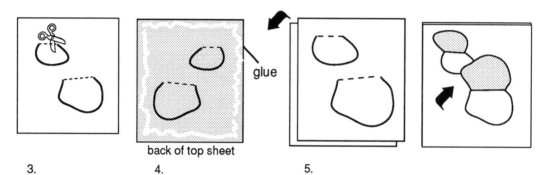

• Masks

Materials: oak tag, patterns, scissors, ice-cream stick or tongue depressor, crayons or markers

To Assemble:
1. Reproduce the patterns on oak tag.
2. Color (if desired) and cut out mask as directed.
3. Glue a stick to the back of the mask as shown in the diagram.

To Use: Hold the mask in front of the face and act like the animal as indicated in the Teacher Pages.

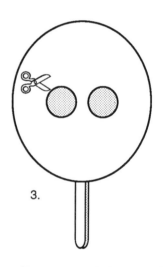

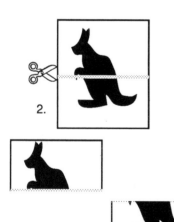

• Match and Sort Cards

Materials: oak tag, card patterns, crayons, scissors, rubber band or envelope

To Assemble:
1. Reproduce the cards on oak tag.
2. Color (if desired) and cut the cards apart.
3. Stack the cards together and secure with a rubber band or store in an envelope.

To Use: Match and sort the cards as indicated on the Teacher Pages in each chapter. After children have learned to match the cards, they may want to create unreal animals by sorting the cards in different ways. Encourage children to describe and name the animals they have made up. Variation: Make a concentration game using the same cards. For this game do not cut cards in half.

• Mini-Books

Materials: white paper, mini-book pattern, scissors, stapler, crayons or markers

To Assemble:
1. Reproduce the mini-book on paper.
2. Color the pictures, if desired.
3. Cut out the pages on the heavy black lines.
4. Fold on dash lines. (See Illustrations below).
5. Staple together with the cover on the front and the back cover on the back.

To Use: Read the book or refer to the pictures to learn about a specific animal.

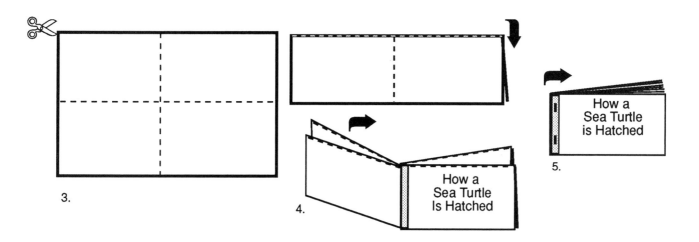

• Nest Builder Board

Materials: Cardboard or a sturdy paper plate, thread and string (have children bring old spools of yarn, thread, and string from home), dryer lint, hole punch, 12" cord or yarn, non-toxic glue, scissors.

To Make:
1. Cut slits around the edge of the cardboard.
2. Put 6-8" lengths of thread or string into the slits, leaving the ends to hang down.
   Note: Soft yarn can be untwisted and added to the cardboard. Also, try bright colors and sparkling threads. Notice which ones birds prefer!
3. Glue the dryer lint (for birds to use inside their nests) to the center of each side of the board.
4. Punch a hole at one edge and tie to a tree branch with a yarn or cord.

To Use: Birds will fly by and take the strings and lint to build their nests.

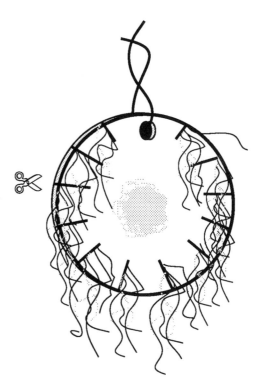

• Peek-a-Boo Facts

Materials: oak tag, patterns, scissors, glue, crayons or markers

To Assemble:
1. Reproduce the patterns on oak tag.
2. Color (if desired) and cut out patterns.
3. Glue the center of the top to the center of the bottom in area shown on pattern.
4. Glue facts in place below illustrations. You may want to add your own facts instead.

To Use: Lift the flaps and read the facts. Children may want to make up questions about the facts and ask other children to answer them.

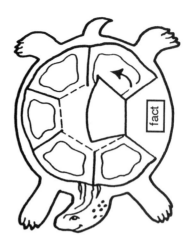

• Pencil Toppers

Materials: oak tag, pencil topper patterns, scissors, hole punch, crayons or markers, pencils

To Assemble:
1. Reproduce the topper patterns on oak tag.
2. Color, if desired.
3. Cut out pencil toppers and punch holes on black circles.
4. Thread bottom hole, then top hole over the eraser end of a pencil.

• Picture Cubes

Materials: oak tag, picture cube patterns, crayons, scissors, clear tape, or glue

To Assemble:
1. Reproduce cube patterns on oak tag.
2. Color and cut out cubes.
3. Fold into a box shape as shown. Tuck in flaps.
4. Tape or glue edges to secure.

To Use: After the cubes are assembled, children move them around to match both ends of the animals pictured on the sides of the cubes. After they have matched the cubes correctly, they may want to create unreal animals by mixing the cubes from other chapters. Encourage them to give a descriptive name to their unusual animals.

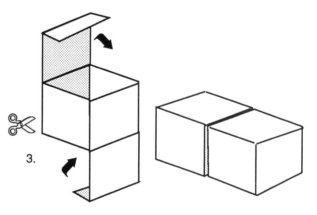

• Pop-Up Cards

Materials: oak tag, patterns, scissors, glue, crayons or markers

To Assemble:

1. Reproduce the patterns on oak tag.
2. Color them, if desired.
3. Cut out all the pieces.
4. Fold on dash lines.
5. Glue the animal patterns to the card in the areas shown on the card (see diagram).

To Use: Close the card and open it to make the animal pop up. Add a fact to remember, or a short poem to make an award or greeting card.

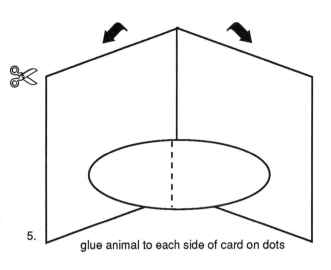

5.

glue animal to each side of card on dots

• Theatres in the Round with Puppets

Materials: oak tag, theatre/puppet patterns, crayons, scissors, glue, ice-cream sticks

To Reproduce:

1. Reproduce all the patterns on oak tag. Enlarge them (if you like) to make a more dramatic impact with your classroom displays and play productions.

To Assemble the Theatres:

2. Color the scenes.
3. Glue the short strips together at one end to make a long strip.
4. Glue the long strip behind the background at each side (as shown) to make the theatre stand up and provide a circular stage in front. **Note:** The rain forest theatre is glued at the side edges to make a circular scene (see diagram below).

To Assemble the Puppets: Enlarge puppets to be in proportion to the theaters (if desired). There are three types of puppets:

Finger Puppets: Color, cut out, adjust tabs to fit fingertips. Glue tabs in place.

Stick Puppets: Color, cut out, and glue a wooden stick to the back.

Standing Puppets: Color, cut out, and fold to stand.

To Use: Move the puppets in and out of the theatre, telling a story about the scene or naming the animals in the scene. Use the information in the activity section and other materials to create songs, poems, or simple puppet plays about the various theater environments.

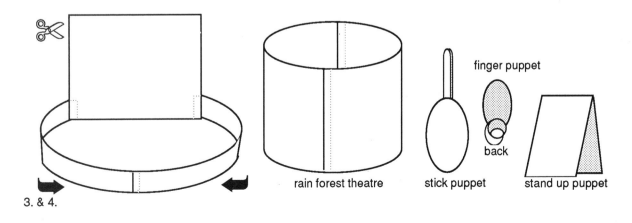

3. & 4.

rain forest theatre   stick puppet   stand up puppet

finger puppet

back

Bibliography

Use this list as a starting point to finding resources to bring into your classroom. Contact your local librarian for help in finding these and other books appropriate for your classroom. Look for other titles featuring animal camouflage, defense, homes, migration, reproduction, family life, food chain, and hunting.

Reference Books

Animals in Winter (National Geographic, 1982)

Animals of Course! by Jill Bailey (G. P. Putnam's Sons, 1984)

Baby Animals by John Bennett Wexo (Creative Editions, 1986)

Baby Animals by Richard Roe (Random House, 1985)

Hands-On Nature: Information and Activities for Exploring the Environment with Children (Vermont Institute of Natural Science, 1986)

Jungle Animals by Angela Royston (Aladdin Books, 1990)

Mysteries and Marvels of the Animal World by Karen Goaman (Usborne Publishing, 1985)

Nature All Year Long by Clare Walker Leslie (Greenwillow Books, 1991)

Our Amazing Animal Friends by Judith Rinard (National Geographic, 1990)

The Random House Book of 1001 Questions and Answers About Animals by Elizabeth Fagan (Rand McNally, 1990)

The Simon and Schuster Young Reader's Book of Animals (Simon and Schuster, 1991)

Wild Animals of North America edited by Thomas P. Allen (National Geographic, 1979)

Zoo Animals by Aladdin Books (Aladdin Books, 1991)

Mammals

Animal Builders by Kenneth Lilly (Random House, 1984)

A First Look at Mammals by Millicent Selsam (Scholastic Book Services, 1973)

Mammals and How They Live by Robert M. McClung (Random House, 1963)

Pandas by John Bennett Wexo (Creative Editions, 1989)

Small Mammals and Where to Find Them by Helen Tee-Van (Knoph, 1966)

Usborne First Nature: Wild Animals by Barbara Cook (Usborne, 1982)

Whales by Kath Buffington and Maria Fleming (Scholastic, 1992)

The World of Whales by Sarah Palmer (Derrydale Books, Random House, 1990)

Amphibians

Common Frog by Oxford Scientific Films (Putnam's, 1979)

A First Look and Frogs, Toads and Salamanders by Millicent Selsom and Joyce Hunt (Walker 1976)

A Frog's Body by Joanna Cole (Morrow, 1980)

Reptiles

Crocodile and Alligator and Lizard by Vincent Serventy (Animals in the Wild Series, Raintree, 1984)

Crocodiles and Alligators by Kate Petty (Watts, 1985)

Green Turtle Mysteries by John T. Waters (Crowell, 1972)

A New True Book: Reptiles by Lois Ballard (Children's Press, 1982)

What Is a Reptile? by Susan Kuchalla (Troll, 1982)

Birds

Baby Birds and How They Grow by Jane R. McCavley (National Geographic, 1983)

Birdsong Lullaby by Diane Stanley (Morrow, 1985)

Eagles by John Bennett Wexo (Creative Editions, 1989)

Flocks of Birds by Charlotte Zolotow (Crowell, 1981)

Just Two Wings by J. E. Givens (Atheneum, 1984)

Owls by John Bennett Wexo (Creative Editions, 1987)

Usborne First Nature—Birds by Rosamund Kidman Cos and Barbara Cox (Usborne, 1980)

When Birds Change Their Feathers by Roma Gans (Crowell, 1980)

A Year of Birds by Ashly Wolff (Dodd, Mead, 1984)

Wetlands
Alligator by Jack Denton Scott (Putnam, 1984)

Between Cattails by Terry Tempest Williams (Scribner's, 1985)

The Everglades: Exploring the Unknown by Christopher Linn (Troll, 1976)

Explore A Spooky Swamp by Wendy W. Cortesi (National Geographic Society, 1976)

Swamp Spring by Carol and Donnald Carrick (Macmillan, 1969)

Year on Muskrat Marsh by Berniece Freschet (Scribner's, 1974)

Posters of Florida wetlands can be ordered from: Tropical Nature Services, Rt. 1, Box 860, Micanopy, FL 32667

Oceans
Animals of the Sea by Millicent E. Selsam (Four Winds, 1975)

The Crab on the Seashore by Jennifer Coldrey (Stevens, 1987)

Edge of the Sea by Russell Sackett (Time-Life, 1983)

The Sea , a Wonder Starters Book (Grosset & Dunlap, 1974)

When the Tide Is Low by Shiela Cole (Lothrop, Lee, & Shepard, 1985)

Rain Forests
Jungles by Illa Podendorf (Children's Press, 1982)

The Jungles: A Science Activity Book (Puffin, 1987)

Life in the Rainforests by Lucy Baker (Franklin Watts, 1990)

Rain Forest Homes by Althea (Cambridge University Press, 1985)

Save the Rainforest Poster can be ordered from: Rainforest Action Network, 301 Broadway, Suite A, San Francisco, CA 94133

The Tropical Rain Forest Set (slides and booklet available from: Educational Images Ltd., P.O. Box 3456, West Side, Elmira, NY 14905)

Deserts
The Desert: What Lives There by Andrew Bronin (Coward, McCann and Geoghegan, 1972)

Deserts by Carroll R. Norden (Raintree Children's Books, 1978)

Deserts, A New True Book by Elsa Posell (Children's Press, 1982)

Wonders of the Desert by Louis Sabin (Troll, 1982)

Endangered Animals
The Animal Kingdom: Endangered Animals by Malcolm Penny (Bookwright Press, 1988)

Endangered Animals by Dean Morris (Raintree Press, 1984)

More Information and Classroom Materials
Carolina Biological Supply Company, 2700 York Rd. Burlington, NC 27215. This company has records and other science materials for the classroom.

Local zoos, nature centers, and museums.

Nature With Children of All Ages by Edith Sisson (Massachusetts Audubon, 1982)

Project WILD, the Western Regional Environment Education Council, Salina Star Route, Boulder, CO 80302

Science Series Publishing Co., 3550 Durock Rd. Shingle Springs, CA 95682. Science kits with song cassettes, flash cards, games, and crafts.

State and local colleges and universities (departments of biology and zoology.)

Index